SOFTWARE ENGINEERING DESIGN

D. Rama Lakshmi
Assistant Professor,
Dept of CSE, Sathyabama Institute
of Science and Technology

R. Ramya
Assistant Professor,
Dept of CSE, Sathyabama Institute
of Science and Technology

T.G. Ruby Angel
Assistant Professor,
Dept of CSE, Sathyabama Institut
of Science and Technology

KHANNA BOOK PUBLISHING CO. (P) Ltd.
4C/4344, Ansari Road, Darya Ganj,
New Delhi, India

Sathyabama Institute of Science and Technology
Jeppiaar Nagar, Rajiv Gandhi Salai,
Chennai, Tamilnadu, India

Dear Readers,

To prevent the piracy, this book is secured with HIGH SECURITY HOLOGRAM on the front title cover. In case you don't find the hologram on the front cover title, please write us to at contact@khannabooks.com or whatsapp us at +91-99109 09320 and avail special gift voucher for yourself.

Specimen of Hologram on front Cover title:

Moreover, there is a SPECIAL DISCOUNT COUPON for you with EVERY HOLOGRAM.

How to avail this SPECIAL DISCOUNT:

Step 1: Scratch the hologram
Step 2: Under the scratch area, your "coupon code" is available
Step 3: Logon to www.khannabooks.com
Step 4: Use your "coupon code" in the shopping cart and get your copy at a special discount
Step 5: Enjoy your reading!

Thanks,
Khanna Publishing House

ISBN: 978-93-55384-27-0

Software Engineering Design
by **D. Rama Lakshmi; R. Ramya; T.G. Ruby Angel**

First Edition: 2026

To view complete list of books, please scan the QR Code:

Published by:
Khanna Book Publishing Co. (P) Ltd.
CIN: U22110DL1998PTC095547

Visit us at: www.khannabooks.com
Write us at: contact@khannabooks.com

Printed in Bharat.

Preface

Software engineering design is the foundation upon which successful software systems are built. As technology advances and software applications become more complex, the need for well-structured, scalable, and maintainable designs has never been greater. This book aims to provide a comprehensive exploration of software engineering design principles, methodologies, and best practices, equipping students and professionals with the knowledge necessary to create robust software solutions.

This book is structured to cater to both beginners and experienced software engineers. It covers fundamental concepts, design patterns, architectural principles, and modern software development practices. Readers will gain insights into the importance of software modeling, requirement analysis, system design, and the impact of emerging technologies on software engineering.

The goal of this book is not only to provide theoretical knowledge but also to bridge the gap between theory and practical application. Through real-world examples, case studies, and hands-on exercises, readers will develop a deeper understanding of how software design choices influence system performance, security, and maintainability.

I would like to express my gratitude to the numerous professionals, educators, and researchers whose contributions to the field have shaped the content of this book. I hope this resource serves as a valuable guide for students, educators, and practitioners alike, fostering a deeper appreciation for the art and science of software engineering design.

Contents

SOFTWARE LIFE CYCLE MODELS

1

UNIT

Software Life Cycle Models

Software Life Cycle Models (SLCMs) provide a structured framework for planning, developing, testing, deploying, and maintaining software systems. These models help ensure efficient project management by defining stages and processes that guide software development.

Traditional models like the **Waterfall Model** follow a sequential, phase-wise approach, making them suitable for projects with well-defined requirements but less adaptable to changes. The **V-Model** (Verification and Validation Model) improves upon this by integrating testing at each development phase, ensuring early defect detection.

More flexible models, such as the Incremental Model and **Spiral Model**, allow iterative development, making them ideal for evolving requirements. **Agile methodologies**, including Scrum and Kanban, focus on adaptability, continuous feedback, and customer collaboration, enabling faster development cycles.

The **Rapid Application Development** (RAD) Model prioritizes rapid prototyping and user involvement for quick iterations. Modern approaches like DevOps emphasize automation, continuous integration, and deployment, ensuring seamless collaboration between development and operations teams. The choice of a software life cycle model depends on factors like project complexity, risk management, and business needs, ensuring successful and efficient software development.

1.1 Definition of Software Life Cycle Models

A **Software Life Cycle Model (SLCM)** is a structured approach that defines the various stages of software development, from initial planning to deployment and maintenance. It provides a systematic framework for managing software projects by outlining the processes, methodologies, and workflows required to develop high-quality software efficiently. Different models, such as Waterfall, Agile, Spiral, and DevOps, offer unique approaches to handling project requirements, risk management, and development timelines. The choice of a life cycle model depends on project complexity, flexibility needs, and business objectives.

1.2 Benefits of a Well-Defined Software Life Cycle Model

A well-defined Software Life Cycle Model (SLCM) ensures a structured and efficient approach to software development, leading to high-quality outcomes and successful project execution. It provides better project management, ensuring proper planning, resource allocation, and risk mitigation. **Higher software quality** is achieved through systematic development and rigorous testing at each phase, reducing defects and enhancing reliability.

Additionally, a structured model helps in cost and time efficiency by minimizing rework and optimizing workflows. Models like Spiral and Agile offer better risk management by identifying and addressing potential issues early. A clear life cycle also enhances collaboration and communication among developers, testers, and stakeholders, ensuring smooth coordination.

Furthermore, a structured approach improves scalability and maintainability, making future updates and modifications easier. Ultimately, a well-defined life cycle model leads to greater customer satisfaction by delivering software that meets user expectations while ensuring compliance with industry standards and security requirements.

A well-defined Software Life Cycle Model (SLCM) provides a structured approach to software development, ensuring efficiency, quality, and successful project execution. The key benefits include:

- Improved Project Management
- Higher Software Quality
- Efficient Time and Cost Management
- Better Risk Management
- Enhanced Collaboration and Communication
- Scalability and Maintainability
- Customer Satisfaction
- Regulatory Compliance

Improved Project Management

A well-defined Software Life Cycle Model (SLCM) enhances **project management** by providing a structured framework for planning, execution, and monitoring. It ensures **clear project objectives**, defining requirements, scope, and deliverables from the start. **Better resource allocation** is achieved by assigning tasks, estimating costs, and managing time effectively. **Risk management** becomes more efficient as potential issues are identified and addressed in early development phases.

Additionally, a structured approach ensures **smooth coordination and collaboration** among teams, improving communication between developers, testers, and stakeholders. Progress tracking and milestone-based development help **in better monitoring and control,** ensuring timely delivery and adherence to project goals.

By following a systematic life cycle model, organizations can reduce project failures, optimize productivity, and ensure successful software development within budget and schedule constraints.

These features contribute to better control, reduced risks, and successful project execution, making software development more efficient and reliable.

Higher Software Quality

A well-defined Software Life Cycle Model (SLCM) ensures **higher software quality** by integrating structured processes, rigorous testing, and best practices throughout development. It enhances **code reliability** by following systematic development phases, reducing errors and inconsistencies. Continuous **quality assurance (QA) and testing** at every stage help detect defects early, preventing costly rework later.

Additionally, adherence to **industry standards and best practices** ensures compliance with security, performance, and scalability requirements. Well-structured documentation and version control further enhance maintainability and long-term software stability. By promoting **user feedback and iterative improvements**, models like Agile and DevOps ensure that the final product meets customer expectations.

Ultimately, a well-defined SLCM leads to **fewer defects, better performance, and a more reliable software product**, increasing user satisfaction and business success.

Efficient Time and Cost Management

A well-defined Software Life Cycle Model (SLCM) optimizes **time and cost management** by providing a structured approach to development, minimizing inefficiencies, and reducing unnecessary expenses.

1. Time Management Benefits

- Structured Planning & Scheduling
- Parallel Development & Iterative Approaches
- Automation & Process Optimization
- Early Risk Detection & Issue Resolution

Structured Planning & Scheduling

Structured **planning and scheduling** in a **Software Life Cycle Model (SLCM)** ensure a well-organized and efficient development process. It provides a clear roadmap by defining project objectives, deliverables, and timelines. Through milestone-based progress tracking, task prioritization, and resource allocation, teams can effectively manage workloads and avoid delays.

By integrating realistic time estimation, risk assessment, and adaptive scheduling, software projects remain on track while accommodating changes. Tools like Gantt charts, Kanban boards, and sprint tracking enhance visibility and accountability. Ultimately, structured planning and scheduling lead to efficient time management, cost savings, improved collaboration, and timely delivery of high-quality software.

Parallel Development & Iterative Approaches

Parallel development and iterative approaches play a crucial role in modern software life cycle models by enabling faster development, flexibility, and continuous improvement. In parallel development, different teams work on independent modules or features simultaneously, reducing overall project timelines. This approach relies on modular design, version control systems like Git, and effective team collaboration to ensure seamless integration.

Iterative approaches focus on incremental development, where software is built in small cycles, tested frequently, and refined based on continuous feedback. Agile methodologies, such as Scrum, emphasize breaking development into sprints, allowing teams to adapt quickly to changing requirements. These approaches help in early risk identification, faster issue resolution, and improved software quality by incorporating customer feedback throughout the process.

Benefits of Parallel Development & Iterative Approaches

- Faster development and time-to-market.
- Improved flexibility and adaptability to changes.
- Early risk identification and issue resolution.
- Higher software quality through continous refinement.

By combining **parallel development and iterative methods**, organizations can accelerate time-to-market, enhance software reliability, and ensure their products align with evolving business and user needs.

Automation & Process Optimization in Software Life Cycle Models

Automation and process optimization are essential in modern software life cycle models, enhancing efficiency, reducing manual effort, and improving overall software quality. **Automation** involves using tools and scripts to streamline repetitive tasks such as code integration, testing, deployment, and monitoring. **Continuous Integration/Continuous Deployment (CI/CD)** pipelines automate code merging, testing, and deployment, ensuring faster and more reliable software releases. Automated **testing frameworks** detect bugs early, reducing rework and improving software stability.

Process optimization focuses on refining workflows, eliminating bottlenecks, and improving resource utilization. Agile and DevOps methodologies emphasize **automated workflows, collaboration, and iterative improvements** to enhance productivity. By integrating **AI-driven analytics, predictive monitoring, and cloud-based infrastructure**, organizations can further optimize performance and scalability. Ultimately, **automation and process optimization** lead to **reduced development time, lower costs, higher accuracy, and faster time-to-market**, making software development more efficient and adaptive to changing business needs.

Early Risk Detection & Issue Resolution in Software Life Cycle Models

Early risk detection and issue resolution are critical for ensuring software quality, reducing project failures, and minimizing costs. A well-defined **Software Life Cycle Model (SLCM)** incorporates risk assessment and issue resolution strategies at every stage of development. By identifying potential riskssuch as security vulnerabilities, performance bottlenecks, or requirement mismatchesearly in the process, teams can implement mitigation strategies before they escalate into major problems.

Techniques like automated testing, static code analysis, and real-time monitoring help detect issues early, ensuring timely resolution. Agile methodologies, DevOps practices, and Continuous Integration/Continuous Deployment (CI/CD) pipelines enable frequent testing, rapid feedback, and iterative improvements, reducing defects and improving software stability. Risk assessment frameworks, such as Failure Mode and Effects Analysis (FMEA) and risk-based testing, further enhance issue detection.

2. Cost Management Benefits

- Efficient Resource Allocation
- Reduced Rework & Maintenance Costs
- Scalability & Future-Proofing
- Optimized Budgeting & Forecasting

Efficient Resource Allocation

Efficient resource allocation ensures that human, technical, and financial resources are optimally utilized throughout the Software Life Cycle Model (SLCM) to maximize productivity and minimize waste. Proper allocation involves assigning the right personnel to tasks based on expertise, ensuring that development tools and infrastructure are used effectively, and managing budgets to prevent cost overruns.

Key strategies include workload balancing, task prioritization, and real-time monitoring to prevent bottlenecks and optimize efficiency. Agile and DevOps methodologies promote dynamic resource management, enabling teams to adapt to changing requirements. Automation tools further streamline resource usage by reducing manual efforts in testing, deployment, and monitoring.

By implementing **efficient resource allocation**, organizations can improve team productivity, accelerate project timelines, reduce costs, and ensure smooth software development and maintenance.

Reduced Rework & Maintenance Costs

A well-structured **Software Life Cycle Model (SLCM)** minimizes **rework and maintenance costs** by emphasizing early issue detection, rigorous testing, and efficient planning. By following best practices such as **requirement validation, automated testing, and continuous integration**, teams can identify and address defects in the early stages, reducing the need for costly rework later.

Proactive strategies like **code reviews, risk assessment, and modular development** ensure that software is built with scalability and maintainability in mind. Agile and DevOps methodologies promote **frequent iterations and real-time feedback**, allowing for continuous improvements without major overhauls. Additionally, well-documented code and structured software architecture make future updates easier and more cost-effective.

Scalability & Future-Proofing

Scalability and future-proofing are essential aspects of modern software development, ensuring that applications can handle increasing workloads and adapt to future technological advancements. A well-defined Software Life Cycle Model (SLCM) incorporates scalable architectures, flexible design patterns, and modular development to accommodate growth without requiring major rework.

Scalability focuses on designing software that can efficiently handle increased user demands, data loads, and system complexities. This is achieved through cloud computing, microservices architecture, database optimization, and load balancing.Future-proofing ensures that software remains relevant and adaptable by integrating extensible frameworks, backward compatibility, and support for emerging technologies. Agile methodologies and DevOps practices promote continuous updates, reducing the risk of technological obsolescence.

Optimized Budgeting & Forecasting

Optimized budgeting and forecasting in a Software Life Cycle Model (SLCM) ensure efficient financial planning, cost control, and resource allocation throughout the development process. By accurately estimating costs at each phase such as planning, development, testing, deployment, and maintenance organizations can prevent budget overruns and maximize return on investment (ROI).

Effective budgeting involves identifying key cost drivers, such as personnel, infrastructure, and tools, while leveraging cost-saving strategies like cloud-based solutions, automation, and Agile methodologies. Forecasting uses data analytics, historical trends, and risk assessment to predict future expenses and resource needs, helping teams adjust plans proactively.

Better Risk Management

Better risk management in a Software Life Cycle Model (SLCM) ensures that potential challenges and uncertainties are identified, assessed, and mitigated early in the development process. Risks in software projects can arise from requirement changes, technical failures, security vulnerabilities, budget overruns, or schedule delays. A structured SLCM incorporates risk assessment frameworks, proactive monitoring, and mitigation strategies to prevent these issues from impacting project success.

Techniques such as Failure Mode and Effects Analysis (FMEA), risk-based testing, and automated monitoring help detect and address risks early. Agile and DevOps methodologies enhance adaptability by allowing teams to respond quickly to emerging threats.

Additionally, continuous feedback loops, stakeholder communication, and contingency planning further strengthen risk management.

Enhanced Collaboration and Communication

Enhanced collaboration and communication play a crucial role in the success of software development projects by ensuring seamless interaction between teams, stakeholders, and clients. A well-defined Software Life Cycle Model (SLCM) promotes structured workflows, clear documentation, and effective coordination, reducing misunderstandings and improving productivity.

Agile and DevOps methodologies emphasize cross-functional teamwork, daily stand-up meetings, and real-time feedback, enabling faster decision-making and adaptability to changes. Collaboration tools like JIRA, Slack, Trello, and Confluence facilitate efficient task management, document sharing, and communication among remote or distributed teams.

Scalability and Maintainability

Scalability and maintainability are key factors in software development that ensure a system can handle growth efficiently while remaining easy to update and manage over time. A well-structured Software Life Cycle Model (SLCM) incorporates scalable architectures and maintainable code practices to extend the software's longevity and adaptability. Scalability ensures that software can accommodate increased user loads, data growth, and evolving business needs.

This is achieved through cloud computing, microservices architecture, database optimization, and load balancing, allowing seamless performance even as demands increase.

Maintainability focuses on designing software that is easy to modify, debug, and upgrade. Best practices like modular programming, code documentation, version control, and automated testing simplify updates and reduce technical debt. Agile and DevOps methodologies enhance maintainability by promoting continuous integration, automated deployments, and iterative improvements.

Customer Satisfaction

Customer satisfaction is a key objective in software development, ensuring that the final product meets user expectations, needs, and quality standards. A well-structured Software Life Cycle Model (SLCM) enhances customer satisfaction by emphasizing requirement analysis, iterative development, rigorous testing, and continuous feedback loops throughout the development process.

Agile and DevOps methodologies prioritize frequent user engagement, incremental improvements, and rapid issue resolution, ensuring that the software aligns with evolving customer requirements. Features like user-friendly interfaces, performance optimization, security enhancements, and reliable support services further contribute to a positive user experience.

Regulatory Compliance

Regulatory compliance ensures that software development adheres to industry standards, legal requirements, and security guidelines to protect users, data, and business operations. A well-defined Software Life Cycle Model (SLCM) incorporates compliance measures at every stage, from requirement gathering to deployment and maintenance.

Compliance frameworks like GDPR (General Data Protection Regulation), HIPAA (Health Insurance Portability and Accountability Act), ISO 27001, and PCI-DSS (Payment Card Industry Data Security Standard) set rules for data protection, security, accessibility, and ethical software practices. Adhering to these standards minimizes legal risks, prevents data breaches, and enhances customer trust.

1.3 Generic Phases of the Software Life Cycle Model

A **Software Life Cycle Model (SLCM)** follows a structured approach to software development, ensuring efficiency, quality, and scalability. The **generic phases** of an SLCM define key stages in the software development process:

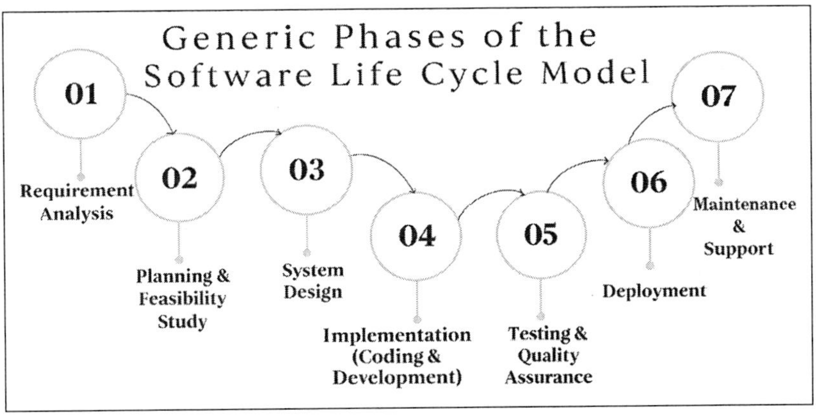

Figure 1.1

Requirement Analysis

Requirement Analysis is the first and most critical phase in the Software Life Cycle Model (SLCM), ensuring that the software meets business needs and user expectations. This phase involves gathering, documenting, and analyzing functional and non-functional requirements from stakeholders, including clients, end-users, and regulatory bodies.

Importance of Requirement Analysis

- Prevents misunderstandings and project failures.
- Reduces development rework and costs.
- Ensures alignment between user needs and final product.
- Enhances software scalability and maintainability.

A well-executed **requirement analysis** phase sets the foundation for successful software development by minimizing risks and ensuring a clear, structured roadmap.

Planning & Feasibility Study

The Planning & Feasibility Study phase is crucial in a Software Life Cycle Model (SLCM) as it ensures that the project is viable, cost-effective, and aligned with business goals before development begins. This phase helps in defining the scope, estimating resources, identifying risks, and determining whether the project should proceed.

Importance of Planning & Feasibility Study

- Prevents unnecessary costs and project failures.
- Ensures efficient use of resources and time.
- Reduces risks by identifying challenges early.
- Provides a clear roadmap for successful execution.

A well-executed Planning & Feasibility Study ensures that software development starts on a strong foundation, reducing uncertainties and increasing the chances of projectsuccess.

System Design

The System Design phase in a Software Life Cycle Model (SLCM) involves creating a blueprint for how the software will function and be structured. This phase transforms the requirements gathered in the previous stages into a detailed architecture, ensuring that the system meets performance, security, and usability expectations.

Key Components of System Design

1. **High-Level Design (HLD):** Defines the overall system architecture, including:
   - System modules and their interactions.
   - Database structures and storage mechanisms.
   - Technology stack selection (programming languages, frameworks, and tools).
   - System security, scalability, and performance considerations.
2. **Low-Level Design (LLD):** Provides detailed specifications for each component, including:
   - Algorithm designs and data flow diagrams.
   - Class diagrams, function definitions, and interface details.
   - Error handling, logging mechanisms, and security protocols.

Key Activities in the System Design Phase

- Creating system architecture diagrams and technical specifications.
- Defining database schemas, APIs, and user interface (UI) layouts.
- Ensuring security, scalability, and maintainability considerations.
- Reviewing and validating designs before development begins.

Importance of System Design

- Reduces development errors and rework by providing a clear roadmap.
- Improves system efficiency, scalability, and maintainability.
- Ensures alignment with business goals and user needs.
- Facilitates seamless collaboration between development, testing, and deployment teams.

A well-defined **System Design phase** ensures that software development is structured, efficient, and adaptable to future needs, leading to a high-quality and scalable final product.

Implementation (Coding & Development)

The **Implementation (Coding & Development)** phase in a **Software Life Cycle Model (SLCM)** is where the actual software is built based on the system design specifications. Developers translate the system architecture into working code by writing, compiling, and integrating software components.

Key Activities in the Implementation Phase

- **Code Development:** Writing code using the selected programming languages and frameworks.
- **Version Control & Collaboration:** Using tools like **Git, GitHub, or GitLab** to manage source code and track changes.
- **Unit Testing:** Developers test individual modules to verify functionality before integration.
- **Code Review & Optimization:** Ensuring that the code follows best practices for efficiency, security, and maintainability.
- **Module Integration:** Combining individual components to create a complete system.
- **Bug Fixing & Debugging:** Identifying and resolving errors to ensure stability.
- **Documentation:** Creating technical documentation for future maintenance and enhancements.

Importance of the Implementation Phase

- Converts system design into a functional product.
- Ensures reliability, security, and efficiency in the software.
- Reduces future maintenance costs by following best practices.
- Prepares the system for integration, testing, and deployment.

A well-structured **Implementation (Coding & Development) phase** ensures that the software is robust, scalable, and aligned with business objectives, setting the stage for successful testing and deployment.

Testing & Quality Assurance

Testing and Quality Assurance (QA) are critical components of the Software Life Cycle Model (SLCM) that ensure the software meets functional, performance, security, and usability requirements before deployment.

While Testing focuses on detecting and fixing defects, Quality Assurance ensures that development processes prevent defects in the first place.

Difference Between Testing & Quality Assurance

Feature	Testing	Quality Assurance (QA)
Definition	Process of executing software to find defects.	Ensures that development processes prevent defects.
Focus	Product-oriented (validates the software functionality).	Process-oriented (improves development standards).
Objective	Detects and fixes bugs before deployment.	Ensures compliance with quality standards and best practices.
Timing	Conducted after development (during verification & validation).	Continuous process throughout the software life cycle.
Methods Used	Manual & automated testing, functional & non-functional testing.	Process audits, documentation reviews, and adhrence to standards.

Types of Software Testing

- Functional Testing (Verifies What the System Does)
- Non-Functional Testing (Verifies How the System Performs)

Functional Testing

Functional Testing is a software testing process that ensures an application functions as per the specified requirements. It verifies user inputs, system outputs, UI behavior, APIs, and overall functionality. Common types include unit testing, integration testing, system testing, and user acceptance testing (UAT), conducted manually or using automation tools like Selenium and JUnit.

This testing helps detect defects early, improving software reliability and user experience. By ensuring the software meets business and technical requirements, functional testing plays a crucial role in delivering a high-quality product.

Non-Functional Testing

Non-Functional Testing evaluates a software system's performance, security, usability, and scalability rather than its core functionalities. It includes Performance Testing (speed and responsiveness), Security Testing (vulnerability assessment), Usability Testing (user-friendliness), and Compatibility Testing (cross-platform support).

This testing ensures the software is efficient, secure, and reliable under various conditions. Automated tools like JMeter, LoadRunner, and OWASP ZAP are commonly used for execution. By conducting non-functional testing, organizations enhance software quality, ensuring a seamless user experience and compliance with industry standards.

Quality Assurance (QA) Practices

- QA Strategies
- Tools for Testing & QA

QA Strategies

Quality Assurance (QA) Strategies focus on improving software development processes to prevent defects and ensure high-quality products. Key strategies include process standardization (following industry best practices like ISO and CMMI), automated testing (using tools like Selenium and JUnit for efficiency), and code reviews (ensuring adherence to coding standards).

- **Process Standardization:** Follows industry standards (ISO, CMMI, Six Sigma).
- **Code Reviews & Peer Reviews:** Ensures coding best pratices are followed.
- **Automated Testing & CI/CD:** Uses tools like Selenium, JUnit, and Jenkins for efficiency.
- **Defect Tracking & Root Cause Analysis:** Identifies issues and prevents recurrence.

Tools for Testing & QA

Tools for Testing & Quality Assurance (QA) play a vital role in ensuring software reliability, functionality, and performance. These tools help automate testing, track defects, and improve overall software quality. Test management tools like JIRA, TestRail, and QTest assist in organizing test cases and tracking progress. Automation testing tools such as Selenium, Appium, and TestNG streamline repetitive tests, reducing manual effort.

- **Test Management:** JIRA, TestRail, QTest.
- **Automation:** Selenium, Appium, JUnit, TestNG.
- **Performance Testing:** JMeter, LoadRunner.
- **Security Testing:** OWASP ZAP, Burp Suite.

Importance of Testing & QA

A well-defined Testing & Quality Assurance strategy ensures that software is delivered with high quality, minimal defects, and optimal performance, ultimately leading to a successful and sustainable product.

- Ensures software reliability, security, and high performance.
- Reduces defects, minimizing post-deployment maintenance costs.
- Improves customer satisfication by delivering bug-free software.
- Enhances compliance with industry regulations and standards.

Deployment – Releasing the Software to Users

Deployment is the final phase of the software development life cycle (SDLC), where the fully tested software is released to users. This process ensures that the application is installed, configured, and made accessible in the production environment. Deployment can be carried out in different strategies, including phased rollout (gradual release to specific user groups), blue-green deployment (switching between two environments to minimize downtime), canary deployment (testing with a small group before full release), and big bang deployment (releasing the software to all users at once).

Effective deployment requires careful planning, automation, and monitoring to ensure a smooth transition with minimal disruptions. Tools like Docker, Kubernetes, Jenkins, and Ansible help automate deployment, while monitoring solutions like New Relic and Prometheus track system performance post-release. A successful deployment ensures software stability, performance, and a seamless user experience, with rollback plans in place to address unexpected issues.

Maintenance & Support

Maintenance & Support is a critical phase of the Software Development Life Cycle (SDLC) that begins after deployment. It involves updating software, fixing post-deployment issues, and enhancing features to keep the system functional, secure, and efficient. This phase ensures that the software continues to meet user needs, remains compatible with evolving technologies, and adheres to industry regulations.

Software maintenance is categorized into four types: Corrective Maintenance (fixing bugs and defects), Adaptive Maintenance (modifying software for new environments or regulations), Perfective Maintenance (enhancing performance and usability), and Preventive Maintenance (proactively identifying and addressing potential issues). Organizations use issue tracking and monitoring tools like JIRA, ServiceNow, and Splunk to manage bug fixes and system updates efficiently.

A well-structured **Maintenance & Support** strategy helps **reduce downtime, improve user satisfaction, and extend the software's lifespan**, ensuring continued business success.

These phases ensure **structured development, risk mitigation, and high-quality software delivery**, making the process efficient and adaptable to changing requirements.

1.4 Verification and Validation in Software Life Cycle Management

Verification and Validation (V&V) are essential quality assurance processes in Software Life Cycle Management (SLCM) that ensure the software is developed correctly and meets user requirements. These processes are integrated into different phases of the Software Development Life Cycle (SDLC) to prevent defects, reduce costs, and enhance overall software quality.

1. Verification in Software Life Cycle Management
2. Validation in Software Life Cycle Management

1. Verification in Software Life Cycle Management

Verification in Software Life Cycle Management (SLCM) is the process of ensuring that software development activities and deliverables conform to specified requirements, standards, and best practices. It is a process-oriented approach that focuses on reviewing documents, designs, and code before actual testing begins. The goal of verification is to identify errors early in the software development life cycle (SDLC), reducing defects, rework, and costs.

Key Activities in Verification

- **Requirement Reviews:** Ensuring that requirements are clear, complete, and consistent.

- **Design Reviews:** Evaluating architectural and system designs for feasibility and correctness.
- **Code Reviews & Static Analysis:** Checking source code for errors, adherence to coding standards,
- **Walkthroughs & Inspections:** Peer reviews of software documents and deliverables to detect defects early.
- **Test Plan & Case Reviews:** Verifying that test plans and test cases align with software requirements.

Importance of Verification in SLCM

- **Detects defects early**, reducing costly fixes in later stages.
- **Ensures compliance** with industry standards and regulations.
- **Improves software quality** by following best practices and structured development processes.
- **Enhances development efficiency**, minimizing rework and delays.

Verification Across Software Development Life Cycle (SDLC) Phases

SDLC Phase	Verfication Activities
Requirement Analysis	Reviewing requirement documents, identifying inconsistencies, and ensuring clarity.
System & Software Design	Validating architecture, UI/UX, and database design before development.
Implementation (Coding)	performing code reviews, static analysis, and ensuring coding standards.
Testing Preparation	Reviewing test cases, test strategies, and defect-tracking mechanisms.
Deployment & Maintenance	Checking configuration settings, reviewing monitoring tools, and ensuring documentation completeness.

By integrating Verification into Software Life Cycle Management, organizations can ensure a structured, defect-free, and high-quality software development process, leading to successful project outcomes.

2. Validation in Software Life Cycle Management

Validation in Software Life Cycle Management (SLCM) is the process of ensuring that the final software product meets user requirements, business needs, and intended functionality. Unlike Verification, which checks if the software is built correctly, Validation ensures that the right software is built. It is a product-oriented process performed through different testing techniques to confirm that the software functions correctly in real-world scenarios.

Key Activities in Validation

- **Unit Testing:** Verifying individual components or modules for correctness.
- **Integration Testing:** Ensuring different modules work together as expected.
- **System Testing:** Checking the overall functionality, performance, and security.

- **User Acceptance Testing (UAT):** Validating the software with end-users before deployment.
- **Performance & Security Testing:** Assessing the software's efficiency, scalability, and vulnerability to security threats.

Validation Across Software Development Life Cycle (SDLC) Phases

SDLC Phase	Verfication Activities
Requirement Analysis	Confirming that the requirement align with user expectations.
System & Software Design	Validating that the design meets functional and business needs.
Implementation (Coding)	performing unit tests to ensure individual components work as expected.
Testing	Executing functional, system, and performance tests to validate behavior.
Deployment & Maintenance	Conducting UAT, monitoring software performance, and validatin updates.

Importance of Validation in SLCM

- **Ensures the software meets user expectations** and business objectives.
- **Reduces post-deployment defects**, leading to fewer production issues.
- **Enhances software usability, security, and performance** through real-world testing.
- **Improves customer satisfaction** by delivering a reliable and high-quality product.

By integrating Validation in Software Life Cycle Management, organizations can ensure that the software is fully functional, meets business goals, and provides a seamless user experience before release.

Integration of V&V in Software Life Cycle Phases

SDLC Phase	Verfication Activities	Validation Activities
Requirement Analysis	Requirement reviews, feasibility analysis	Validating requirements with stakeholders
System & Software Design	Architectural and UI reviews prototyping	Validating design meets functional needs
Implementation (Coding)	Code reviews, static analysis, unit tests	Validating developed features through functional testing
Testing Preparation	Test plan reviews, defect tracking	System testing, integration testing. UAT
Deployment & Maintenance	Configuration reviews monitoring setup	Validating system stability, bug fixes, and performance checks

Importance of Verification & Validation in SLCM

- **Prevents defects early**, reducing development costs.

- **Improves software reliability and performance.**
- **Enhances compliance** with industry standards and regulations.
- **Increases customer satisfaction** by ensuring the final product meets expectations.

By implementing Verification and Validation (V&V) in Software Life Cycle Management, organizations can ensure software quality, minimize risks, and improve overall project success.

Software Life Cycle Models

- Waterfall model
- Prototyping model
- RAD model
- Spiral model
- Agile methodologies.

1.5 Waterfall Model

The Waterfall Model is a sequential and linear software development methodology where each phase is completed before moving on to the next. It follows a structured approach, making it easy to manage and document. This model is best suited for projects with clearly defined requirements that are unlikely to change.

- It is one of the oldest models in SDLC.
- It is the mother of all model.

Phases of the Waterfall Model

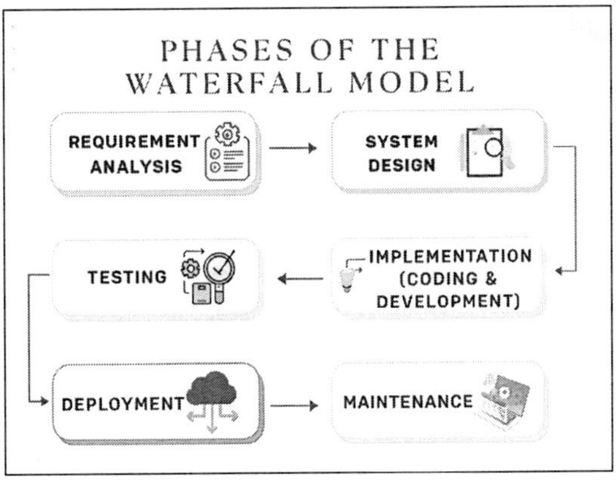

Figure 1.2

Requirement Analysis

Requirement Analysis is the first and most crucial phase of the Software Development Life Cycle (SDLC). It involves gathering, analyzing, documenting, and validating the functional and non-functional requirements of the software. This phase ensures that the final product meets business objectives and user expectations.

Key Activities in Requirement Analysis

- **Requirement Gathering:** Collecting information from stakeholders, clients, and end-users.
- **Requirement Documentation:** Writing Software Requirement Specification (SRS) documents.
- **Requirement Validation:** Ensuring completeness, clarity, and feasibility.
- **Requirement Prioritization:** Identifying critical features and functionalities.
- **Requirement Review & Approval:** Getting confirmation from stakeholders before proceeding.

Types of Requirements

- **Functional Requirements:** Define what the system should do (e.g., user authentication, data processing).
- **Non-Functional Requirements:** Define system qualities (e.g., performance, security, scalability).
- **Business Requirements:** Define high-level objectives and business goals.
- **User Requirements:** Define what the end-users expect from the system.

Importance of Requirement Analysis

- Prevents misunderstandings and ensures alignment with business goals.
- Reduces development time and cost by avoiding rework.
- Improves software quality by clearly defining expectations.
- Enhances stakeholder satisfaction by delivering the right product.

A well-executed Requirement Analysis phase is critical for successful software development, ensuring that all stakeholders are on the same page before moving forward.

System Design

System Design is the phase in the Software Development Life Cycle (SDLC) where the architecture, components, interfaces, and data flow of the system are defined. It serves as a blueprint for developers, ensuring that the software is structured efficiently and meets the specified requirements.

Key Activities in System Design

- **High-Level Design (HLD):** Defines the overall system architecture, including modules, databases, and communication flow.
- **Low-Level Design (LLD):** Details the internal structure of each module, including algorithms, data structures, and class designs.
- **User Interface (UI) Design:** Creates wireframes, mockups, and design elements for user interaction.
- **Database Design:** Defines tables, relationships, and indexing strategies for efficient data storage and retrieval.
- **Security and Performance Considerations:** Implements authentication, authorization, and optimization strategies.

Types of System Design

- **Architectural Design:** Defines the system structure, modules, and interaction
- **Interface Design:** Describes how different system components interact with each other.
- **Data Design:** Organizes data models, schemas, and database architecture.
- **Component Design:** Specifies detailed implementation for each module.

Importance of System Design

- Provides a clear roadmap for developers to follow.
- Ensures scalability, maintainability, and security of the software.
- Reduces development risks by addressing technical challenges early.
- Improves collaboration between designers, developers, and stakeholders.

A well-planned System Design phase ensures efficient development, high performance, and successful project execution while minimizing risks and potential issues.

Implementation (Coding & Development)

Implementation (Coding & Development) is the phase in the Software Development Life Cycle (SDLC) where developers write and integrate the actual code based on the System Design specifications. This phase transforms design documents into a working software application by following coding standards, best practices, and programming guidelines.

Key Activities in Implementation Phase

- **Setting Up the Development Environment:** Configuring tools, frameworks, databases, and repositories.
- **Writing Code:** Developing modules, functions, and integrating APIs based on the design.
- **Unit Testing:** Testing individual components to ensure correctness.
- **Code Review & Optimization:** Conducting peer reviews and optimizing performance.
- **Version Control & Documentation:** Using Git, SVN, or other version control systems to track changes and maintain documentation.

Best Practices for Implementation

- **Follow Coding Standards:** Use Consistent naming conventions, formatting, and documentation.
- **Module & Scalable Code:** Write reusable and scalable code for easier maintenance.
- **Error Handling & Logging:** Implement error detection, logging, and exception handling mechanisms.
- **Security Considerations:** Use encryption, authentication, and secure coding techniques to prevent vulnerabilities.
- **Continous Integration & Deployment (CI/CD):** Automate testing and deployment to streamline the process.

Importance of the Implementation Phase

- Ensures software reliability and performance through testing and optimization.
- Ensures software reliability and performance through testing and optimization.
- Reduces future maintenance costs by following best practices.
- Facilitates smooth integration with other system components.

The **Implementation Phase** is critical for delivering high-quality software that meets business and user requirements while ensuring efficiency, security, and scalability.

Testing

Testing is a critical phase in the Software Development Life Cycle (SDLC) that ensures the software functions correctly, meets requirements, and is free of defects. This phase involves unit testing, integration testing, and system testing, each serving a specific purpose in identifying and resolving issues before deployment.

Key Types of Testing

- Unit Testing
- Integration Testing
- System Testing

1. Unit Testing

Tests individual components or modules to verify their correctness

Unit Testing is a software testing method that verifies individual components or modules to ensure they function correctly. It is performed by developers during the implementation phase using automated frameworks like JUnit, PyTest, or NUnit. Unit testing helps detect bugs early, improves code quality, and simplifies debugging, leading to more reliable and maintainable software.

2. Integration Testing

Validates interactions between integrated modules

Integration Testing ensures that different modules or components of a software system work together correctly. It detects issues like data mismatches, incorrect API calls, and communication failures between integrated units. Common approaches include Top-Down, Bottom-Up, and Big Bang Testing, using tools like Selenium and JUnit. This testing phase helps improve system reliability and functionality before full system deployment.

Testing the data flow between two or more depended module

Example

- Whenever send an Email to another person and that person received a same email is known as Integration testing.
- Searching the product in Flipkart (I phone) and click the search button the next page should shows only I phone is known as integration testing.
- Sending 5000 in Paytm to friend and check whether the same amount is debited and credited is known as integration testing.
- Once functional and integration is completed, we go for system testing.

3. System Testing

Evaluates the complete system's functionality, performance, and security.

System Testing is a software testing phase that evaluates the entire system's functionality, performance, and security to ensure it meets the specified requirements. It verifies that all integrated components work together as expected in a real-world environment.

This testing includes functional, performance, security, and usability testing, using tools like Selenium, JMeter, and Test Complete. By identifying system-wide defects, System Testing ensures software stability and reliability before deployment.

Testing an application from end to end like real user in testing sever limitation to production server.

Example

- Verify by opening Flipkart, search the item, add to cart, make payment, logout.
- Verify by opening Email, sending message, see sent box, logout.
- Verify by opening Email, login, click on setting, select privacy, click password change new password, logout and login with new password.

Importance of Testing in SDLC

- Identifies defects early, reducing cost and effort in later stages.
- Improves software reliability, security, and performance.
- Ensures compliance with business and user requirements.
- Enhances user satisfaction by delivering a stable and error-free product.

By incorporating Unit, Integration, and System Testing, software teams ensure that the final product is high-quality, robust, and meets all functional and non-functional requirements before deployment.

Deployment

Releasing the software to the production environment: Deployment is the process of releasing the fully tested software to users, either in phases or as a full rollout. It involves setting up the production environment, configuring servers, and ensuring smooth installation. Deployment strategies like Blue-Green, Rolling, and Canary Releases help minimize risks and downtime, ensuring a seamless transition for users.

Maintenance

Providing updates, bug fixes, and enhancements as needed: Maintenance is the ongoing process of updating software to fix bugs, improve performance, and add new features after deployment. It includes corrective, adaptive, perfective, and preventive maintenance to ensure the software remains reliable and efficient. Regular maintenance helps enhance user experience, security, and compatibility with evolving technologies.

Advantages of the Waterfall Model

- Simple and easy to understand, with clear documentation.
- Well-structured approach ensures each phase is completed before proceeding.
- Best for stable projects where requirements are well-defined from the start.
- Easy to manage due to its rigid, phase-by-phase progression.

Disadvantages of the Waterfall Model

- Not flexible - changes in requirements are difficult to accommodate.
- Late testing - defects are found after the coding phase, making fixes expensive.
- Not suitable for complex or evolving projects, as requirements must be fully defined upfront.

When to Use the Waterfall Model?

- Projects with stable, well-defined requirements.
- Small to medium-scale projects where predictability and structure are important.
- Industries like banking, defence, and healthcare, where documentation and compliance are crucial.

While the Waterfall Model is one of the oldest software development approaches, it is now often replaced by Agile and Iterative models for dynamic and evolving projects. However, it remains relevant for structured, well-defined, and documentation-heavy projects.

1.6 Prototyping Model

It is a dummy model and is non-working application.

When Do We Go For This Model?

- When the customer is not clear about requirement.
- When the software company is new to the domain, then they will go for prototype model.
- When the developers are new to the technologies.
- When the customer and software company are new to the business.

Explain

The Prototyping Model is an iterative software development approach where a preliminary version (prototype) of the software is built, tested, and refined based on user feedback before final development. This model helps developers and stakeholders visualize requirements early, reducing misunderstandings and ensuring the final product meets expectations.

Phases of the Prototyping Model

Requirement Gathering - Initial requirements are collected, focusing on core functionalities.

The goal of requirement gathering in the prototyping model is to compile the first, high-level requirements needed to create a working prototype. Stakeholders offer input on the prototype, iteratively improving requirements rather than outlining every element up front. This method ensures that the finished program meets expectations, minimizes misconceptions, and helps users understand their needs through ongoing.

Figure 1.3

Quick Prototype Development

Quick Prototype Development is the phase where a basic, working model of the software is created with limited features to demonstrate core functionalities. This prototype is built rapidly using simple UI elements and essential logic to help stakeholders visualize the system early. The goal is not to develop a fully functional product but to gather feedback for improvements. By iterating on the prototype based on user input, developers refine requirements, enhance usability, and ensure the final software meets user expectations efficiently.

Main Features of Quick Prototype Development

- Rapid Development
- Iterative Refinement
- User-Centric Approach
- Cost-Effective
- Limited Functionality

Rapid Development

Rapid Development refers to the fast creation of a basic prototype with minimal coding and essential functionalities. The focus is on speed rather than perfection, allowing stakeholders to interact with an early version of the software. This approach helps identify requirements, detect potential issues, and refine the design through quick iterations, ultimately reducing development time and costs.

Iterative Refinement

Iterative Refinement is the process of continuously improving the prototype based on stakeholder feedback. After each review, necessary modifications are made to enhance functionality, design, and usability. This cycle of testing and updating helps in identifying requirements more accurately, reducing misunderstandings, and ensuring that the final software aligns with user expectations.

User-Centric Approach

The **User-Centric Approach** focuses on designing the prototype with the end-user's needs and experience in mind. It ensures that stakeholders can interact with an early version of the software, provide feedback, and influence improvements. By prioritizing usability, intuitive interfaces, and real-world functionality, this approach enhances user satisfaction and ensures the final product meets expectations.

Cost-Effective

Cost-Effectiveness in **Quick Prototype Development** comes from early issue detection and reduced rework. By creating a basic prototype and refining it iteratively based on user feedback, developers avoid costly changes in later stages. This approach minimizes resource wastage, improves requirement clarity, and ensures that only necessary features are developed, ultimately saving both time and money.

Limited Functionality

Limited Functionality means that the prototype includes only essential features needed to demonstrate the core concept of the software. It focuses on basic workflows, user interactions, and key functionalities without implementing full-scale logic or complex features. This approach allows for quick development, early feedback collection, and iterative improvements, ensuring the final product meets user expectations efficiently.

User Evaluation & Feedback

User Evaluation & Feedback is a crucial phase where stakeholders interact with the prototype to assess its functionality, usability, and overall design. Users provide insights on improvements, missing features, or necessary changes, helping refine requirements. This iterative process ensures the final software aligns with user expectations, reducing errors, minimizing rework, and enhancing overall satisfaction before full-scale development.

Features of User Evaluation & Feedback

- Real-User Interaction
- Requirement Validation
- Iterative Improvement
- Early Issue Detection

Real-User Interaction

Stakeholders and end users actively test the prototype as part of Real-User Interaction to evaluate its overall design, functionality, and usability. Users may examine important features, spot gaps, and offer insightful feedback thanks to this practical experience. Early user involvement helps engineers understand user needs, which improves refinements and guarantees that the finished product is simple to use.

Requirement Validation in User Evaluation & Feedback

A prerequisite Prior to full-scale development, validation makes that the prototype satisfies user needs and commercial objectives. Developers can verify whether the implemented functionalities meet expectations by getting input from stakeholders. By identifying missing or ambiguous requirements early on, this method helps avoid expensive revisions later on and guarantees that the finished product successfully accomplishes its original purpose.

Iterative Improvement in User Evaluation & Feedback

The ongoing process of improving the prototype in response to user input is known as iterative improvement. The necessary adjustments are made to improve overall performance, usability, and functionality following each evaluation. Prior to full-scale development, this cycle of testing and upgrading makes sure that the finished program meets user expectations, lowers errors, and enhances overall quality.

Refinement & Iteration

Refinement & Iteration is the process of continuously improving the prototype based on user feedback and testing results. Each iteration involves analyzing stakeholder input, making necessary modifications, and re-evaluating the system to ensure it meets requirements. This cycle helps in identifying gaps, enhancing usability, and refining functionalities, leading to a well-structured and user-friendly final product.

Features of Refinement & Iteration

- Continuous Improvement
- User-Driven Modifications
- Requirement Adaptability

- Enhanced Usability

Continuous Improvement in Refinement & Iteration

Continuous Improvement is the ongoing process of enhancing the prototype by incorporating feedback and making necessary adjustments. Each iteration refines functionality, usability, and performance, ensuring the software evolves to meet user needs. This approach minimizes errors, enhances user experience, and leads to a more polished and effective final product.

User-Driven Modifications in Refinement & Iteration

User-Driven Modifications involve making changes to the prototype based on direct feedback from stakeholders and end-users. This ensures that the software aligns with real user needs, improving functionality, usability, and overall satisfaction. By continuously refining the system through user input, the final product becomes more intuitive, efficient, and tailored to its intended audience.

Requirement Adaptability in Refinement & Iteration

Requirement Adaptability refers to the ability to modify and refine software requirements as user needs evolve during the development process. It ensures that the prototype remains flexible, allowing adjustments based on stakeholder feedback and changing business goals. This adaptability helps in minimizing misunderstandings, improving system functionality, and delivering a final product that meets real-world expectations.

Final Development & Deployment in the Prototyping Model

Final Development & Deployment is the stage where the refined prototype is transformed into a fully functional software system and released to users. After multiple iterations and feedback cycles, the finalized design and functionalities are implemented with robust coding, thorough testing, and performance optimizations. Once development is complete, the software is deployed using suitable strategies like phased rollout, full deployment, or cloud-based distribution. Proper deployment ensures a smooth transition for users, minimal downtime, and efficient system integration.

Features of Final Development & Deployment

- Fully Functional Software
- Thorough Testing
- Optimized Performance
- Deployment Strategies
- User Training & Support

Fully Functional Software in Final Development & Deployment

Fully Functional Software means that the final product is developed with all required features, integrations, and optimizations, ensuring it meets business and user requirements. It is built based on the refined prototype, incorporating feedback from previous iterations. The software undergoes thorough testing to ensure stability, security, and usability, making it ready for real-world deployment and use.

Thorough Testing in Final Development & Deployment

Thorough Testing ensures that the software is stable, secure, and performs as expected before deployment. It includes various testing levels such as unit testing, integration testing, system testing, and user acceptance testing (UAT) to identify and fix defects. This process helps in delivering a high-quality, reliable, and error-free final product, ensuring a smooth user experience after deployment.

Optimized Performance in Final Development & Deployment

Optimized Performance ensures that the software runs efficiently, with minimal resource consumption and maximum speed. This involves code optimization, database tuning, load balancing, and performance testing to enhance responsiveness and scalability. By refining the system for smooth operation, it improves user experience, reduces downtime, and ensures seamless functionality under varying workloads.

Deployment Strategies in Final Development & Deployment

Deployment Strategies refer to the methods used to release software to end-users while ensuring minimal disruptions and maximum efficiency. The choice of strategy depends on system complexity, user base, and risk factors.

Common deployment strategies include:

- **Full Deployment:** The software is released to all users at once.
- **Phased Deployment:** The release is done in stages, allowing gradual adoption and issue resolution.
- **Blue-Green Deployment:** Two environments (blue and green) run simultaneously, allowing a smooth switch between old and new versions.
- **Rolling Deployment:** The new version is gradually rolled out to small groups before a full release.
- **Canary Deployment:** The software is first released to a small subset of users to test stability before wider rollout.

Each strategy helps manage risks, ensure system stability, and provide a seamless user experience.

User Training & Support in Final Development & Deployment

User Training & Support ensures that end-users can effectively utilize the newly deployed software. Training methods include user manuals, video tutorials, hands-on workshops, and guided onboarding sessions to familiarize users with the system's features. Ongoing support, such as help desks, FAQs, chat support, and troubleshooting assistance, helps resolve issues quickly, ensuring a smooth transition and enhancing user satisfaction.

Advantages of the Prototyping Model

- Improves requirement clarity by allowing users to interact with an early version.
- Reduces development risks by identifying issues early.
- Enhances user satisfaction through continuous feedback and refinements.
- Facilitates better communication between developers and stakeholders.

Disadvantages of the Prototyping Model

- Time-consuming due to multiple iterations and feedback cycles.
- Scope creep risk, as users may request endless changes.
- Higher development costs if too many iterations are needed.

When to Use the Prototyping Model?

- When requirements are unclear and need user validation.
- For complex systems requiring a better user interface or interaction.
- When high user involvement is required for product success.

The Prototyping Model is widely used in UI/UX design, web development, and software requiring frequent user feedback, ensuring a more user-centric final product.

1.7 Spiral Model in Software Development

The Spiral Model is a risk-driven software development process that combines iterative development with systematic risk analysis. It is ideal for large, complex projects where requirements evolve over time. The model follows a cyclical approach, progressing through multiple iterations (or spirals), each consisting of four key phases.

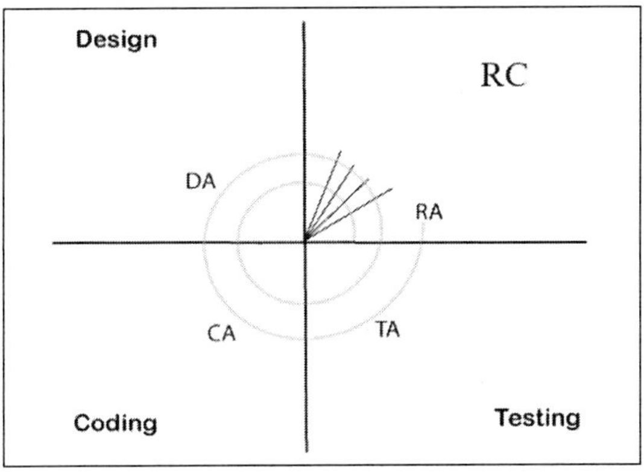

Figure 1.4

Planning in the Spiral Model

The **Planning** phase in the **Spiral Model** focuses on defining objectives, gathering requirements, and identifying constraints for the next development cycle. This includes:

- Understanding user needs and business goals.
- Estimating resources, time, and budget.
- Identifying potential risks that could impact development.
- Defining clear milestones for the upcoming iteration.

This phase ensures that each cycle of the Spiral Model is well-structured, reducing uncertainties and setting a strong foundation for risk analysis and development.

Important Features of the Planning Phase in the Spiral Model

- Requirement Identification

- Risk Assessment
- Resource Allocation
- Milestone Setting
- Stakeholder Involvement

Requirement Identification in the Planning Phase

Requirement Identification is the process of gathering and defining the needs, objectives, and functionalities of the software system. It involves discussions with stakeholders, end-users, and project teams to ensure clarity on expectations and constraints. This step helps in setting a strong foundation for development, reducing ambiguity, and ensuring that the final product aligns with user requirements.

Risk Assessment in the Planning Phase

The process of locating, evaluating, and ranking possible hazards that can have an impact on the software development process is known as risk assessment. It entails assessing operational, financial, and technological risks to determine how they affect project goals. This step lowers the likelihood of unanticipated development failures, ensures smoother project execution, and aids in the creation of risk mitigation techniques.

Resource Allocation in the Planning Phase

The process of resource allocation entails determining and allocating the labor, funds, time, and technology required to guarantee the project's successful completion. It maximizes efficiency and cost-effectiveness while guaranteeing that every stage of development has sufficient resources for seamless advancement. Appropriate resource allocation guarantees timely project completion, prevents overuse, and helps avoid bottlenecks.

Milestone Setting in the Planning Phase

In order to monitor progress and guarantee timely completion, milestone setting entails establishing significant checkpoints in the software development process. Every milestone denotes a noteworthy accomplishment, such as the completion of the prototype, the finalization of the requirements, or successful testing stages. Teams can monitor development progress, stay on track, and make required adjustments to maintain the project in line with goals with the use of these predetermined goals.

Stakeholder Involvement in the Planning Phase

Key players, including customers, end users, project managers, and developers, are guaranteed to actively engage in decision-making through stakeholder involvement. Their input aids in setting priorities, identifying possible dangers early in the process, and fine-tuning needs. By ensuring that the finished product satisfies user expectations, stakeholder engagement increases transparency, aligns development with business objectives, and promotes project success overall.

Risk Analysis in the Spiral Model

The Spiral Model's risk analysis phase is crucial for identifying, assessing, and mitigating possible hazards in the software development process. This entails evaluating project delays, financial limitations, security flaws, and technical difficulties. Then, risk-reduction techniques like feasibility studies, prototypes, and backup plans are created. Continuous risk analysis throughout each iteration keeps the project flexible, lowers the likelihood of failure, and enhances the overall quality of the program.

Main Features of Risk Analysis in the Spiral Model

- Risk Identification
- Risk Evaluation
- Risk Mitigation Strategies

Risk Identification in the Spiral Model

At each iteration of the Spiral Model, risk identification is the process of identifying possible obstacles that could affect software development. These hazards may include security flaws, budgetary restrictions, evolving requirements, and technical limitations. Teams may ensure easier project execution and lower the chance of failures in later stages by proactively developing mitigation plans by recognizing risks early in each cycle.

Risk Evaluation in the Spiral Model

Analyzing the possibility and possible influence of hazards on the software development process is known as risk evaluation. Risks are evaluated in each iteration of the Spiral Model according to technical feasibility, cost, complexity, and timeframe. High-risk components are given priority for mitigation, guaranteeing that important issues are resolved as soon as possible. Making well-informed judgments, lowering uncertainty, and enhancing overall project stability are all aided by this systematic examination.

Risk Mitigation Strategies in the Spiral Model

Risk Mitigation Strategies involve proactive measures to reduce the impact of potential risks during software development. In the **Spiral Model**, these strategies are applied at every iteration to address challenges before they escalate. Common mitigation strategies include:

- **Prototyping:** Building early prototypes to test feasibility and identify issues.
- **Alternative Solutions:** Developing backup plans for high-risk components.
- **Incremental Development:** Implementing small, manageable phases to control risks.
- **Regular Reviews:** Conducting frequent evaluations with stakeholders to detect and resolve risks early.
- **Resource Buffering:** Allocating extra time, budget, or manpower to handle unexpected challenges.

By continuously assessing and mitigating risks, the **Spiral Model** ensures a more **stable, adaptable, and successful** development process.

Engineering (Development & Testing) in the Spiral Model

The Engineering phase in the Spiral Model focuses on developing and testing the software incrementally. Each iteration goes through a structured cycle of design, coding, integration, and validation, ensuring continuous improvements.

- Development
- Testing

Development

The **Development** phase in the **Spiral Model** focuses on designing, coding, and integrating software components in an iterative manner. Each cycle refines and enhances the system based on previous phases.

- **Incremental Coding:** Software is developed in small functional modules, allowing early feedback and adjustments.
- **Prototyping:** Initial versions of the system are created to validate functionality and user requirements.
- **Continuous Refinement:** Code is reviewed and improved based on testing and stakeholder feedback.
- **Integration:** Different components are combined to ensure seamless operation within the overall system.

This iterative development approach ensures higher flexibility, early issue resolution, and better adaptability to changing requirements.

Testing in the Spiral Model

The Testing phase in the Spiral Model ensures that the developed software meets functional and non-functional requirements through rigorous validation at each iteration. Testing is performed throughout the development cycle to identify and fix defects early.

- **Unit Testing:** Individual modules are tested to verify correct functionality.
- **Integration Testing:** Ensures that different modules work together seamlessly.
- **System Testing:** Evaluates the complete system for overall performance and reliability.
- **User Acceptance Testing (UAT):** Involves end-users to validate the software against real-world scenarios.

By incorporating continuous testing in each spiral iteration, the model helps improve software quality, minimize defects, and ensure a stable final product.

When We Go for Spiral Module?

- When customer gives the requirement part by part we go for this model.
- When there is a lot of dependency between the module.

Advantages of Spiral Model

- Customer can see the application partially and can get confidence.
- Requirement changes can be done.
- Compare to waterfall model rework is less.

Drawbacks of Spiral Model

- Testing happens only after coding requirement and design are not tested. λ Developers used to do testing before (currently it is done by test engineer)
- If there is any requirement changes it may delay the project.
- Customer can cancel the project if he is unhappy.

Each cycle results in an improved version of the software, with increasing levels of detail and functionality. This model is highly flexible, allowing for continuous improvements while minimizing risks through early detection and mitigation strategies.

1.8 Agile Methodologies

Agile methodologies are a collection of iterative and incremental software development approaches designed to enhance flexibility, collaboration, and rapid delivery. Unlike traditional models, Agile prioritizes continuous improvement, customer feedback, and adaptability to changing requirements.

Agile development breaks projects into small, manageable iterations (sprints or cycles), allowing teams to deliver working software frequently while incorporating stakeholder feedback. Agile emphasizes team collaboration, customer involvement, and responding to change over rigid planning.

Key Principles of Agile (as per the Agile Manifesto)

Agile development follows **12 key principles** based on the **Agile Manifesto**, promoting flexibility, collaboration, and continuous improvement. The most important principles include.

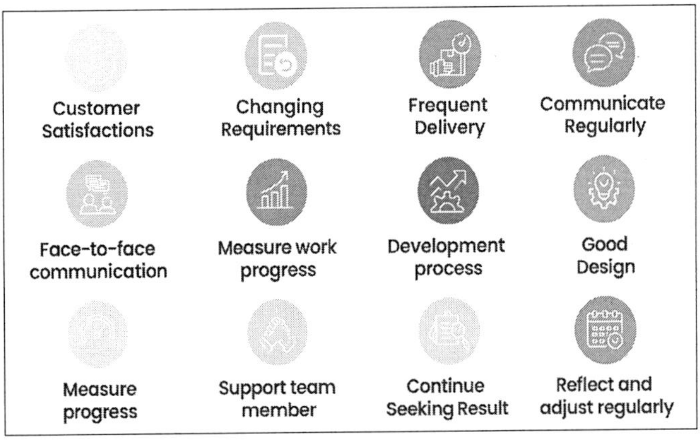

Figure 1.5

1. Customer Satisfaction

This principle concentrates on the importance of customer satisfaction by providing information to customers early on time and also with consistency throughout the development process.

2. Welcome Changing Requirements, Even Late in Development

Agile processes tackle change for the customer's competitive advantage. Even late in development, changes in requirements are welcomed to ensure the delivered software meets the evolving requirements of the customer.

3. Deliver Working Software Frequently

This principle encourages the regular release of functional software increments in short iterations. This enables faster feedback and adaptation to changing requirements.

4. Collaboration between Business Stakeholders and Developers

This says the businesspeople and developers must work together daily throughout the project. There should be communication and collaboration between stakeholders and the development team regularly. This is crucial for understanding and prioritizing requirements effectively.

5. Build Projects around Motivated Individuals

This promotes in giving developers the environment and support they need and trusts them to complete the job successfully. Motivated and empowered individuals are more likely to produce work with quality and make valuable contributions to the project.

6. Face-to-face communication is the Most Effective

Face-to-face communication is the most effective method of discussion and conveying information. This principle depicts the importance of direct interaction which helps minimize misunderstandings, and hence effective communication is achieved.

7. Working Software is the Primary Measure of Progress

This principle emphasizes delivering functional and working software as the primary metric for project advancement. It encourages teams to prioritize the continuous delivery of valuable features, so it ensures that good progress is consistently achieved throughout the process. The primary goal is to provide customers with incremental value and also gather feedback early in the project life cycle.

8. Maintain a Sustainable Pace of Work

Agile promotes sustainable development. All people involved: The sponsors, developers, and users should be able to maintain a constant pace indefinitely. This principle depicts the need for a sustainable and consistent development pace. This helps in avoiding burnout and ensures long-term project success.

9. Continuous Attention to Technical Excellence and Good Design

This principle is on the importance of maintaining high standards of technical craft and design, so it ensures the long-term ability in maintenance and adaptability of the software.

10. Simplicitythe Art of Maximizing the Amount of Work Not Done

Simplicity is essential. The objective here is to concentrate on the most valuable features and tasks and avoid unnecessary complexity as the art of maximizing the amount of work not done is crucial.

11. Self-Organizing Teams

Self-organizing teams provide the best architectures, requirements, and designs. These help in empowering teams to make decisions and organize to optimize efficiency and creativity.

12. Regular Reflection on Team Effectiveness

This makes the team reflect on how to become more effective at regular intervals and then adjust accordingly. Continuous improvement is very crucial for adapting to changing circumstances and optimizing the team's performance over time.

What are Agile Frameworks?

An agile framework is a selected set of practices, roles, artifacts, and activities that help groups implement the agile philosophy in their continuous development tasks, like planning, testing, integration, and other continuous development work. There are many agile frameworks, each with its own strengths, weaknesses, and suitability for specific contexts.

Characteristics of Agile Frameworks

1. **Time-boxed iterations:** They use time-boxed iterations or sprints to supply working software often (commonly every 2-four weeks).
2. **Backlogs:** They use backlogs or lists of prioritized features or personal testimonies to devise and tune the paintings to be achieved.
3. **Daily meetings:** They use daily meetings (generally 15 minutes) to synchronize the group's development and discover any impediments or issues.
4. **Reviews:** They use reviews or demonstrations at the end of each iteration or sprint to show off the working software to customers and stakeholders and acquire comments.
5. **Retrospectives:** They use retrospectives or conferences at the quit of each new release or sprint to reflect on what went well, what can be improved, and what moves to take for the subsequent iteration or dash.

Popular Agile Frameworks

- **Scrum:** Scrum is a popular framework that is used whenever we want to develop complex products, Ken Schwaber and Jeff Sutherland are known as the people who developed Scrum. Scrum is a type of Agile framework.

  Scrum is one of the extensively used agile frameworks. It is primarily based on three pillars:
- Transparency
- Inspection
- Model

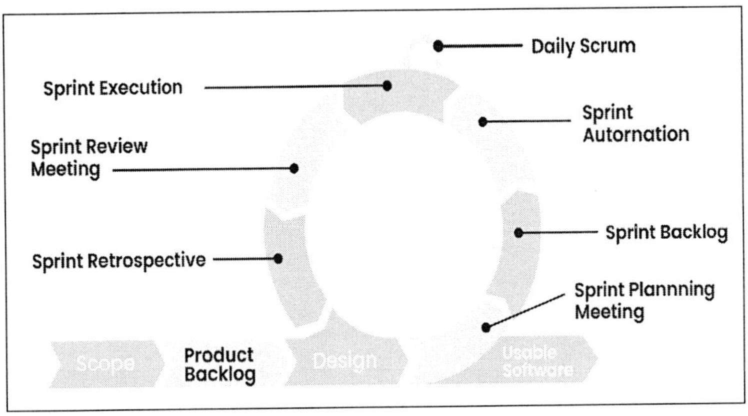

Figure 1.6

- **Scrum defines 3 roles:** the product owner who represents the customer's voice and prioritizes the backlog; the scrum grasp who helps the scrum process and eliminates impediments; and the improvement team supplies doubtlessly shippable increments of software program at the quit of every dash.

Scrum Additionally Defines four Activities

1. **Sprint Planning:** Sprint planning where the crew plans what to do within the subsequent dash. It is a meeting which is conducted before sprint starts. In this meeting product owner and scrum master will be involved. hey will decide which user story has to be worked on that particular sprint. Also, they will decide the duration of the sprint.
2. **Day-by-day:** The day-by-day scrum in which the team updates every other on their progress. All team members will gather together like project manager developer lead , test lead , test engineers , developers , BA. Customer also involves in this meeting. λ Here each employee should give work update every day.

   If the meeting is held in the morning the team members have to convey what they did yesterday and what are they going to do today. If the meeting is held in the evening the team members have to convey what they did today and what are they going to do tomorrow. This is very much helpful for a better communication between team members. Scrum master is the host of this meeting
3. **Dash Review:** The dash review where the group demonstrates the product increment to clients and stakeholders.In this meeting, scrum master will check whether all the user stories are completely developed and tested and is it ready to release customer or not This happens at the end of the sprint.
4. **Sprint Retorspective:** The sprint retrospective in which the crew reflects on a way to enhance their performance.
5. **Sprint backlog:** It is user story which is not completed in that particular sprint that is carried into forward to the next sprint. EX: if 'D' user story is not completed in sprint 1, it is a backlog which taken from sprint1 to sprint2.
6. **Product backlog:**It is the user stories which is taken for a new sprint It is under epic EX : e,f,g,h are from product backlog for sprint 2 In the same way till all the user stories are completed , multiple sprints will be going on and full application will be ready.

Advantage of Scrum Framework

- Scrum framework is fast moving and money efficient.
- Scrum framework works by dividing the large product into small sub-products. It's like a divide and conquer strategy
- In Scrum customer satisfaction is very important.
- Scrum is adaptive in nature because it have short sprint.
- As Scrum framework rely on constant feedback therefore the quality of product increases in less amount of time

Disadvantage of Scrum Framework

- Scrum framework do not allow changes into their sprint.
- Scrum framework is not fully described model. If you wanna adopt it you need to fill in the framework with your own details like Extreme
- Programming(XP), Kanban, Dynamic Systems Development Method (DSDM).
- It can be difficult for the Scrum to plan, structure and organize a project that lacks a clear definition.
- The daily Scrum meetings and frequent reviews require substantial resources.

Kanban

Kanban is a popular Agile Software Development Methodology. It is a signaling device that instructs the moving of parts in a 'pull' production system, developed as part of the TPS (Toyota Production System). Kanban is about envisioning the existing workflow in terms of steps. These steps can be created on the whiteboard.

Key Features of Kanban

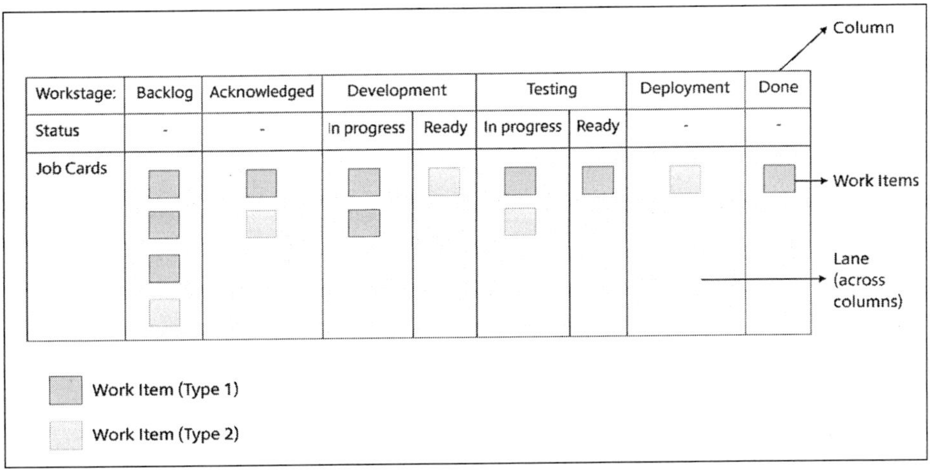

Figure 1.7

Workflow

Backlog -> Acknowledged -> Development -> Testing -> Deployment/UAT -> Done Work stages: Acknowledged, Development (In Progress), Development (Ready), Testing (In Progress), Testing (Ready), Deployment/UAT, Backlog (Arrival Queue), Done (Finished Stage) Work Items: Two types of tasks (Type 1 and Type 2) are represented by work items.

Principles of Kanban

1. **Start with the existing process**: It is a change management method that starts with the existing process. Changes are done in the system in incremental and evolutionary ways. Unlike Scrum, there's no specific process or roles defined in Kanban.

2. **Agree to continue evolutionary and incremental changes:** After starting with the existing process, the team must agree on continuous, incremental, and evolutionary changes. The changes should be small and incremental. Rapid and substantial changes may be effective but they will be subjected to larger resistance as well by the Team.
3. **Admire current roles, processes, responsibilities & titles:** Though Kanban suggests continuous incremental changes in the process, it respects current roles, responsibilities, and job titles. This helps the team to gain confidence as they get started with Kanban.
4. **Leadership at all levels:** Kanban does not expect leadership from a specific set, rather the actions of leadership at all levels in the organization, are very much encouraged.

Kanban is widely used in software development, IT operations, and business process management to increase productivity, enhance team collaboration, and ensure a steady workflow.

1. **Scrume:** Uses sprints (short development cycles) with defined roles like Scrum Master and Product Owner.
2. **Kanban:** Visualizes workflow using boards to track progress and optimize efficiency.
3. **Extreme Programming (XP):** Focuses on coding best practices, test-driven development (TDD), and frequent releases.
4. **Lean Development:** Eliminates waste by maximizing value delivery with minimal resources.
5. **Feature-Driven Development (FDD):** Breaks projects into small, client-valued features for incremental delivery.

Extreme Programming (XP)

Extreme Programming (XP) is an Agile methodology focused on high-quality software development through continuous feedback, collaboration, and best coding practices. It emphasizes short development cycles, frequent releases, and adaptability to changing requirements. XP promotes test-driven development (TDD), pair programming, and continuous integration to ensure software reliability. It encourages close customer involvement to align development with business needs. XP also prioritizes simplicity and refactoring to keep the codebase clean and maintainable.

By following these principles, XP helps teams deliver high-quality software efficiently while responding to changes effectively.

Feature-Driven Development (FDD)

Feature-Driven Development (FDD) is an Agile methodology that focuses on designing, building, and delivering software in feature-based increments. It follows a model-driven approach, emphasizing short development cycles and frequent releases. FDD consists of five key activities: developing an overall model, building a feature list, planning by feature, designing by feature, and building by feature. It encourages team collaboration, scalability, and clear progress tracking. FDD is best suited for large-scale projects where structured yet flexible development is needed to ensure efficiency and maintainability.

Lean Development

Lean Development is an Agile methodology focused on maximizing value while minimizing waste in software development. It emphasizes efficiency, continuous improvement, and delivering high-quality software quickly. Lean follows key principles such as eliminating waste, optimizing learning, empowering teams, and ensuring fast delivery. It encourages iterative development, customer feedback, and adaptive decision-making to enhance productivity. Lean also promotes respect for team members and sustainable work processes. By reducing unnecessary steps and focusing on value-driven features, Lean Development helps create cost-effective, high-performance software solutions.

Agile methodologies help teams deliver high-quality software faster, improve collaboration, and adapt quickly to market changes.

This page is intentionally left blank!

REQUIREMENTS ENGINEERING

2

UNIT

2.1 Understanding Requirements

Requirements Engineering (RE)

Requirements Engineering (RE) is a systematic process of identifying, analyzing, documenting, validating, and managing the needs and constraints of a system to ensure it meets stakeholder expectations. It serves as the foundation of software and systems development, helping to define what a system should do and how it should perform. The process typically includes requirement elicitation, where stakeholders' needs are gathered; analysis and negotiation, where conflicts are resolved; specification, where requirements are formally documented; validation, ensuring accuracy and feasibility; and management, which involves tracking changes throughout the development lifecycle.

RE encompasses both functional and non-functional requirements, along with domain-specific and user needs. Effective RE minimizes project risks, improves software quality, and ensures that development aligns with business goals. However, challenges such as evolving requirements, stakeholder conflicts, and incomplete specifications must be carefully managed through best practices like stakeholder engagement, clear documentation, and traceability techniques.

Phases of Requirements Engineering

Requirements Engineering (RE) consists of several key phases that ensure the successful identification, documentation, and management of system requirements. These phases are:

- Requirements Elicitation
- Requirements Analysis & Negotiation
- Requirements Specification
- Requirements Validation & Verification
- Requirements Management

Requirements Elicitation

This phase involves gathering requirements from stakeholders, users, and domain experts. Techniques such as interviews, surveys, brainstorming, observations, and prototyping are used to understand what is needed from the system. The goal is to identify both functional and non-functional requirements while considering business constraints.

Requirements Analysis & Negotiation

Once the requirements are gathered, they need to be analyzed for completeness, consistency, and feasibility. This phase also involves resolving conflicts between stakeholders by prioritizing requirements based on importance, technical feasibility, and business value. Techniques such as modelling, prototyping, and requirement prioritization methods (e.g., MoSCoW technique) are used.

Requirements Specification

In this phase, the gathered and analyzed requirements are documented in a structured format, such as a Software Requirements Specification (SRS). The specification ensures clarity, correctness, and consistency, allowing developers and stakeholders to have a shared understanding of the system's expected functionality and constraints.

Requirements Validation & Verification

The specified requirements must be validated to ensure they correctly capture stakeholder needs and do not contain inconsistencies, ambiguities, or errors. Validation techniques include reviews, prototyping, testing, and formal inspections. Verification ensures that requirements align with business goals and system constraints.

Requirements Management

This phase involves maintaining and updating requirements throughout the software development lifecycle. As projects evolve, new requirements may emerge, and existing ones may need modifications. Change management, traceability, version control, and impact analysis help ensure that requirements remain relevant and correctly implemented.

Each of these phases plays a critical role in delivering a high-quality system that meets user and business needs while minimizing risks and costly rework.

Functional and Non-Functional

Requirements in Requirements Engineering (RE) are broadly classified into Functional Requirements (FRs) and Non-Functional Requirements (NFRs). Both are essential for a well-designed system, ensuring it performs the right tasks efficiently and effectively.

2.2.1 Functional Requirements (FRs)

Functional Requirements (FRs) define what a system should do by specifying its features, operations, and expected behaviours. They describe how the system processes inputs, responds to user interactions, and fulfills business objectives.

Examples of Functional Requirements

- User Authentication System
- E-commerce Platform
- Banking System
- Healthcare System

User Authentication System

A **User Authentication System** is a security mechanism used to verify the identity of users before granting access to applications, websites, or systems. It ensures that only authorized users can access sensitive data and functionalities.

Key Components of a User Authentication System

- Identification
- Authentication
- Authorization

Identification in User Authentication

Identification is the first step in the User Authentication System, where a user provides a unique identifier to declare their identity to the system. This identifier helps the system recognize who is trying to access it.

Common Identification Methods

- **Username or Email:** Most commonly used for login.
- **User ID or Employee ID:** Unique identifier assigned to users in organizations.
- **Biometric Identifiers:** Such as fingerprints, facial recognition, or retina scans.
- **Smart Cards or Tokens:** Used in secure environments for identity recognition.

Importance of Identification

- Serves as the first layer of security.
- Helps track user activity within a system.
- Ensures users are mapped to the correct access permissions.

After **identification**, the system proceeds to **authentication** to verify the user's claimed identity.

Authentication in User Authentication System

Authentication is the process of verifying a user's identity after they provide an identifier (such as a username or email). It ensures that the person accessing the system is who they claim to be by validating their credentials.

Types of Authentication Methods

- **Password-Based Authentication:** Users enter a password that is checked against stored credentials.
- **Two-Factor Authentication (2FA):** Requires an additional verification step, like an OTP or a security token.
- **Multi-Factor Authentication (MFA):** Uses multiple verification methods (e.g., password + biometric scan + OTP).
- **Biometric Authentication:** Uses fingerprints, facial recognition, or iris scans for verification.
- **Token-Based Authentication:** Uses authentication tokens (e.g., JWT, OAuth) instead of passwords.

Importance of Authentication

- Prevents unauthorized access and protects sensitive data.
- Enhances system security by ensuring only verified users can log in.
- Supports compliance with security standards like **GDPR, HIPAA, and ISO 27001**.

Once authentication is successful, the system proceeds to **authorization**, determining what resources the user can access.

Authorization in User Authentication System

Authorization is the process of determining what actions or resources a user can access after successful authentication. It ensures that authenticated users only have the permissions necessary for their role or privilege level within the system.

Types of Authorization Methods

- **Role-Based Access Control (RBAC):** Assigns permissions based on predefined roles (e.g., Admin, User, Guest).
- **Attribute-Based Access Control (ABAC):** Grants access based on user attributes like department, location, or job title.
- **Discretionary Access Control (DAC):** Allows resource owners to set access permissions for others.
- **Mandatory Access Control (MAC):** Uses strict policies enforced by the system for security-sensitive environments.
- **OAuth & Token-Based Authorization:** Uses tokens (e.g., OAuth, JWT) to grant access to APIs and external services.

Importance of Authorization

- **Ensures data security** by restricting unauthorized access.
- **Prevents privilege escalation** and reduces security risks.
- **Improves system control** by enforcing role-based permissions.

Authorization works after authentication to define and enforce access control policies, ensuring users can only perform allowed actions within a system.

E-commerce Platform

An **E-Commerce Platform** is an online system that enables businesses and individuals to buy and sell products or services over the internet. It provides the necessary tools for managing product listings, payments, customer interactions, and order fulfillment.

Key Components of an E-Commerce Platform

- **Product Catalog:** Manages product listings, descriptions, pricing, and inventory.
- **Shopping Cart & Checkout:** Allows users to select products, review their order, and complete purchases securely.
- **Payment Gateway Integration:** Supports various payment methods like credit/debit cards, PayPal, digital wallets, and cryptocurrencies.
- **User Authentication & Authorization:** Ensures secure login, account management, and role-based access for customers and administrators.

Types of E-Commerce Platforms

- **Business-to-Consumer (B2C):** Online stores like Amazon, eBay, and Shopify-powered websites.
- **Business-to-Business (B2B):** Platforms for wholesale transactions between businesses.
- **Consumer-to-Consumer (C2C):** Marketplaces like eBay and Facebook Marketplace where individuals sell to each other.

Benefits of an E-Commerce Platform

- **24/7 availability**, allowing businesses to operate globally.
- **Cost-effective** compared to physical stores.
- **Personalized shopping experiences** through AI-driven recommendations.
- **Scalability**, enabling businesses to grow without major infrastructure changes.

A well-designed E-Commerce Platform enhances the shopping experience, streamlines operations, and drives revenue growth for businesses.

Banking System

A **Banking System** is a digital infrastructure that enables financial institutions to manage accounts, process transactions, and provide banking services securely and efficiently. It ensures smooth financial operations, customer account management, and regulatory compliance.

Key Components of a Banking System

- Customer Account Management
- Authentication & Security
- Transaction Processing
- Payment Gateway Integration

Customer Account Management in Banking Systems

Customer Account Management is a core function of a banking system that enables financial institutions to create, maintain, and secure customer accounts. It ensures efficient handling of financial transactions, account details, and customer interactions while maintaining regulatory compliance.

Benefits of Customer Account Management:

- **Enhances security** by protecting sensitive financial data.
- **Improves customer experience** with easy access to account details and services.
- **Ensures regulatory compliance** with financial laws and anti-money laundering (AML) policies.
- **Reduces operational costs** through automation and digital banking services.

A well-structured Customer Account Management System ensures secure, efficient, and seamless banking experiences for users while enabling banks to manage financial operations effectively.

Authentication & Security in Banking Systems

Authentication & Security in banking systems ensure that only authorized users can access financial services while protecting sensitive data from fraud and cyber threats. Strong security measures are crucial to prevent unauthorized access, data breaches, and financial fraud.

Benefits of Authentication & Security in Banking

- **Prevents unauthorized access** to sensitive financial data.
- **Enhances customer trust** by ensuring secure banking transactions.
- **Reduces fraud risks** through advanced AI-driven fraud detection.
- **Ensures regulatory compliance** with financial security standards.

A robust Authentication & Security system is essential for protecting users, preventing cyber threats, and ensuring secure online banking experiences.

Transaction Processing

Transaction Processing is a core function of banking systems that handles the execution, validation, and recording of financial transactions in real-time or batch mode. It ensures secure, accurate, and efficient movement of funds between accounts while maintaining compliance with financial regulations.

Benefits of Efficient Transaction Processing

- Ensures fast and accurate transaction execution.
- Enhances customer experience with real-time banking services.
- Reduces fraud risks through secure processing methods.
- Improves operational efficiency and compliance.

A well-optimized transaction processing system is crucial for secure, efficient, and seamless financial operations in modern banking.

Payment Gateway Integration

Payment Gateway Integration is a crucial component of digital banking and e-commerce that enables secure and seamless online transactions. It acts as an intermediary between customers, merchants, and banks to process payments through various methods, ensuring security and compliance with financial regulations.

Security Measures in Payment Gateway Integration

- **End-to-End Encryption (E2EE):** Protects sensitive financial data from breaches.
- **PCI-DSS Compliance:** Ensures secure handling of cardholder data.
- **Tokenization:** Replaces sensitive payment details with unique tokens to prevent data theft.
- **Multi-Factor Authentication (MFA):** Adds an extra layer of security, such as OTP verification.

Benefits of Payment Gateway Integration

- Fast and seamless transaction processing.
- Enhanced security with encryption and fraud detection.

- Supports global payments and multiple currencies.
- Automated transaction tracking and reporting.

A well-integrated payment gateway enhances security, efficiency, and customer experience in digital banking and online transactions.

2.1.2 Non-Functional

Non-Functional Requirements (NFRs) define the quality attributes of a banking system rather than its specific functionalities. These requirements ensure the system is secure, reliable, scalable, and user-friendly, supporting smooth operations under various conditions.

Key Non-Functional Requirements (NFRs)

- Security
- Performance
- Scalability
- Reliability & Availability
- Compliance & Regulatory Standards

Security in Banking Systems

Security is a critical non-functional requirement (NFR) in banking systems, ensuring that financial transactions, user data, and sensitive information are protected against unauthorized access, fraud, and cyber threats. A strong security framework builds customer trust, prevents financial losses, and ensures compliance with banking regulations.

Key Security Measures in Banking Systems

- **Encryption & Data Protection:** Uses SSL/TLS encryption to secure data transmission and protect stored customer information.
- **Multi-Factor Authentication (MFA):** Requires multiple verification methods, such as passwords, OTPs, biometrics (fingerprint, facial recognition), and security tokens.
- **Fraud Detection & Risk Monitoring:** Implements AI-driven fraud detection to analyze transaction patterns and flag suspicious activities.
- **Access Control & Authorization:** Uses role-based access control (RBAC) to restrict system access based on user roles and responsibilities.
- **Compliance with Regulatory Standards:** Adheres to PCI-DSS, GDPR, KYC, and AML regulations to ensure financial security and prevent fraud.

Importance of Security in Banking

- Prevents financial fraud and data breaches.
- Ensures safe and reliable transactions.
- Protects customer identity and sensitive information.
- Maintains regulatory compliance and avoids legal penalties.

A **strong security framework** is essential for ensuring a **safe, reliable, and compliant** banking system.

Performance

Performance is a crucial non-functional requirement (NFR) in banking systems, ensuring that transactions and operations are processed quickly, efficiently, and without delays. High-performance banking systems enhance user experience, support large transaction volumes, and maintain system stability even during peak loads.

Key Performance Factors in Banking Systems

- **Fast Transaction Processing:** Ensures real-time fund transfers, bill payments, and loan processing with minimal delays.
- **High Throughput & Low Latency:** Supports millions of transactions per second with response times in milliseconds.
- **Scalability:** Adapts to growing user demands by efficiently handling increased workloads and concurrent users.
- **Load Balancing & Optimization:** Uses distributed servers and cloud computing to evenly distribute traffic and prevent system slowdowns.
- **Database Performance:** Implements optimized indexing, caching, and query execution to process large volumes of financial data efficiently.

Importance of Performance in Banking

- Enhances customer satisfaction with quick and smooth transactions.
- Supports a high volume of users without system crashes or delays.
- Ensures uninterrupted banking operations even during peak hours.
- Optimizes resource utilization for cost efficiency.

A high-performing banking system ensures seamless, fast, and reliable financial services for users.

Scalability in Banking Systems

Scalability is a key non-functional requirement (NFR) that ensures a banking system can handle increasing workloads, growing user demands, and expanding transaction volumes without performance degradation. A scalable banking system can seamlessly adapt to changes, such as higher traffic, additional services, or expanding customer bases, while maintaining efficiency.

Key Aspects of Scalability in Banking Systems

- **Horizontal & Vertical Scaling:** Supports horizontal scaling (adding more servers) and vertical scaling (upgrading existing infrastructure) to manage growth efficiently.
- **Cloud-Based Architecture:** Leverages cloud computing for flexible resource allocation, ensuring dynamic scalability during peak transaction periods.
- **Load Balancing:** Uses distributed computing and load balancers to evenly distribute requests, preventing server overload and improving response times.
- **Modular & Microservices Architecture:** Breaks down banking services into independent, scalable modules, allowing efficient updates and expansions.
- **Database Scalability:** Implements sharding, indexing, and caching to optimize query performance and manage large volumes of financial data.

Importance of Scalability in Banking

- Handles growing user bases without slowing down services.
- Ensures smooth performance during high-traffic events (e.g., salary processing, Black Friday sales).
- Facilitates easy expansion into new markets and services.
- Optimizes operational costs by scaling resources as needed.

A scalable banking system guarantees long-term efficiency, flexibility, and seamless growth to meet evolving customer and business demands.

Reliability & Availability

Reliability & Availability are critical non-functional requirements (NFRs) that ensure banking systems operate consistently, without failures, and remain accessible to users at all times. These attributes guarantee that financial transactions, customer data, and banking operations are processed accurately and without unexpected downtime.

Key Aspects of Reliability & Availability in Banking Systems

- **99.99% Uptime Guarantee:** Ensures continuous system availability through redundant servers, failover mechanisms, and backup solutions.
- **Fault Tolerance & Disaster Recovery:** Implements automated backups, data replication, and failover strategies to prevent service disruptions.
- **High-Availability Architecture:** Uses load balancing and distributed computing to ensure smooth performance even under heavy traffic.
- **Error Handling & Auto-Recovery:** Detects and corrects system failures, transaction errors, and database inconsistencies without user intervention.
- **Redundant Infrastructure:** Deploys geo-redundant data centers to prevent localized failures from affecting global banking operations.

Importance of Reliability & Availability in Banking:

- Prevents financial losses due to system downtime.
- Ensures customers can access banking services 24/7.
- Enhances trust and confidence in digital banking platforms.
- Reduces risks of transaction failures and data corruption.

A highly reliable and available banking system ensures seamless, uninterrupted, and secure financial operations for users worldwide.

Compliance & Regulatory Standards

Compliance & Regulatory Standards are essential non-functional requirements (NFRs) that ensure banking systems adhere to legal, financial, and security regulations set by governments and financial authorities. Compliance helps protect customer data, prevent fraud, ensure financial transparency, and avoid legal penalties.

Key Compliance & Regulatory Standards in Banking

- **PCI-DSS (Payment Card Industry Data Security Standard):** Ensures secure handling of credit/debit card transactions to protect against fraud and data breaches.

- **GDPR (General Data Protection Regulation):** Protects customer privacy by enforcing strict data security, consent, and transparency policies.
- **KYC (Know Your Customer) & AML (Anti-Money Laundering):** Mandates identity verification to prevent fraud, money laundering, and terrorist financing.
- **SOX (Sarbanes-Oxley Act):** Enforces financial integrity and accountability through proper reporting and auditing processes.
- **Basel III:** Regulates risk management, capital requirements, and liquidity to maintain banking stability.

Importance of Compliance & Regulatory Standards in Banking

- Ensures financial stability and security.
- Protects customer data from cyber threats and fraud.
- Prevents legal risks, fines, and reputational damage.
- Builds customer trust and confidence in banking services.

A compliant banking system ensures secure, transparent, and legally sound financial operations, aligning with global regulatory requirements.

2.1.3 Other Classifications

Apart from the commonly used functional, non-functional, and domain requirements, requirements can also be classified in several other ways based on different perspectives. Here are some alternative classifications.

- Based on Scope & Abstraction
- Based on Changeability
- Based on Priority & Importance

Based on Scope & Abstraction

Classification of Requirements Based on Scope &Abstraction

Requirements can be categorized based on their level of detail and scope within the system development process.

The key levels are:

- Business Requirements
- User Requirements
- System Requirements

Business Requirements in Requirements Engineering

Business requirements define the high-level objectives, goals, and expectations of a project from a business perspective. They focus on why the system is being developed and what business value it should provide.

- **Scope:** Organization-wide
- **Focus:** Business goals, not technical details
- **Audience:** Stakeholders, executives, product managers

Examples of Business Requirements

- The system should improve customer retention by 15% within the next year.
- The platform must automate invoice processing to reduce manual errors by 80%.
- The new mobile app should increase online sales by 25%.
- The system must comply with GDPR and ISO 27001 standards.

How to Gather Business Requirements?

- **Stakeholder Interviews:** Meet with executives, managers, and customers.
- **Surveys & Questionnaires:** Collect feedback from employees or users.
- **Workshops & Brainstorming:** Collaborate to identify business priorities.
- **Market & Competitor Analysis:** Study trends and industry benchmarks.

User Requirements

User requirements define the needs, expectations, and interactions that users have with a system. They focus on what users want to achieve rather than technical details.

- **Scope:** User interactions with the system
- **Focus:** User needs, actions, and experiences
- **Audience:** End-users, UX/UI designers, product managers

Examples of User Requirements

- Users should be able to register using their email or social media accounts.
- Users should receive real-time notifications about order status updates.
- A customer should be able to search for products by category, price range, and ratings.
- The system should allow employees to submit leave requests through a mobile app.

Why Are User Requirements Important?

- Ensure the system is user-friendly and meets real needs.
- Improve user satisfaction and engagement.
- Reduce the risk of usability issues and costly redesigns.
- Align software development with customer expectations.

System Requirements

System requirements define the detailed technical specifications that a system must meet to fulfill business and user needs. They describe how the system should function and operate within a given environment.

- **Scope:** Entire system functionality, architecture, and constraints
- **Focus:** Technical implementation details
- **Audience:** Developers, system architects, QA testers, IT teams

How to Gather System Requirements?

- **Workshops with Developers & Architects:** Discuss technical feasibility.

- **Review Business & User Requirements:** Convert them into technical specs.
- **Industry Standards & Compliance:** Consider GDPR, ISO, HIPAA, etc.
- **Prototyping & Testing:** Validate technical feasibility through POCs (Proof of Concept).

System Requirements Specification (SRS) Document

System requirements are often documented in an **SRS document**, which includes:

- **Introduction:** Purpose, scope, definitions.
- **Overall Description:** System environment, user characteristics.
- **Functional Requirements:** Features, workflows, interactions.
- **Non-Functional Requirements:** Performance, security, scalability.
- **Constraints & Assumptions:** Technical and business limitations.

Based on Priority & Importance

Requirements can be categorized based on their level of priority and importance to the system. This helps stakeholders and developers decide what to implement first and manage resources efficiently.

- **Scope:** Helps in requirement prioritization for development
- **Focus:** Essential vs. optional features
- **Audience:** Product managers, stakeholders, developers

How to Prioritize Requirements?

- **MoSCoW Method:** Categorize as Must-Have, Should-Have, Could-Have, Won't-Have
- **Kano Model:** Classify based on user satisfaction (Basic, Performance, Exciting)
- **Cost-Benefit Analysis:** Prioritize based on value vs. effort
- **Stakeholder Input:** Gather feedback from business, users, and developers

Why is Requirement Prioritization Important?

- Ensures critical functionalities are implemented first.
- Helps manage budget and time constraints effectively.
- Improves agile development by focusing on essential features.
- Reduces risk of scope creep and delays.

2.2 Modelling Requirements

What is Requirements Modeling?

Requirements modelling is the process of visually representing business, user, and system requirements to improve clarity, communication, and analysis. These models help stakeholders and developers understand, validate, and refine requirements before implementation.

- **Scope:** Covers business processes, system behaviors, and user interactions.

- **Focus:** Converting textual requirements into structured diagrams and models.
- **Audience:** Business analysts, developers, project managers, stakeholders.

Comparison of Requirements Modeling Techniques

Technique	Purpose	Best For
Use Case Diagram	Shows user interactions	Functional requirements, system behavior
Data Flow Diagram (DFD)	Shows data movement	Process modeling, inpur/output analysis
ER Diagram (ERD)	Trpresents data relationships	Database design, data managment
State Transition Diagram	Models system states	UI navigation, state-driven processes
BPMN	Represents workflows	Business process automation, approvals

Why is Requirements Modeling Important?

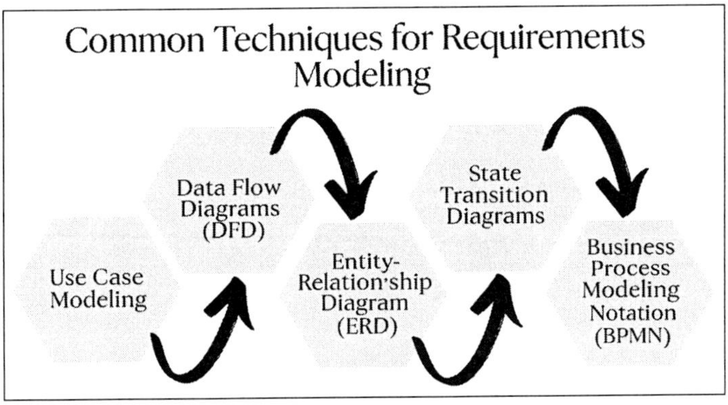

Figure 2.1

- Improves clarity by visualizing complex requirements.
- Enhances stakeholder communication by using simple diagrams.
- Reduces errors by validating requirements before development.
- Supports Agile & Waterfall methodologies by refining requirements.

Use Case Modeling in Requirements Engineering

Use case modeling is a visual representation of how users (actors) interact with a system to achieve specific goals. It helps define the system's functional requirements by showing different scenarios, user roles, and system responses.

- **Scope:** User interactions with the system
- **Focus:** Functional requirements and system behavior
- **Audience:** Business analysts, developers, testers, stakeholders

Key Components of a Use Case Model

Actors

- External entities that interact with the system.
- Can be **humans, external systems, or devices**.
- **Example:** "Customer," "Admin," "Payment Gateway API."

Use Cases

- Describes an **action** or functionality the system provides.
- **Example:** "Place Order," "Login," "Generate Report."

System Boundary

- Defines what is **inside** and **outside** the system.
- Helps clarify **scope and interactions**.

Relationships

- **Association**: Direct interaction between actors and use cases.
- **Include (<<include>>)**: A mandatory dependency between use cases.
- **Extend (<<extend>>)**: An optional/conditional use case extension.
- **Generalization**: An actor or use case inherits behavior from another.

Example

```
+-------------------------------------+
|          Online Shopping System     |
|                                     |
|  (👤 Customer) -----> [Search Products]        |
|                                     |
|  (👤 Customer) -----> [Place Order] --------> [Process Payment] <<include>>
|                                     |
|  (👤 Admin) -----> [Manage Inventory]        |
+-------------------------------------+
```

Actors

- Customer
- Admin

Use Cases

- Search Products
- Place Order
- Process Payment (<<include>>)
- Manage Inventory

Relationships

- **<<include>>** → "Process Payment" is a required step in "Place Order."

Use Case Description Template

Field	Description
Use Case Name	Login
Actors	Customer
Preconditions	User must have a registered account
Basic Flow	1. User enters credentials 2. System validates input 3. User is logged in
Alternative Flow	1. Invalid credentials → Display error message
Postconditions	User is redirected to the dashboard

Benefits of Use Case Modeling

- Clarifies functional requirements for developers and stakeholders.
- Improves communication between technical and business teams.
- Enhances test case development by defining expected system behaviors.
- Helps scope project boundaries and avoid unnecessary features.

2.2.1 Data Flow Diagram (DFD)

Data Flow Diagram (DFD) represents the flow of data within information systems. Data Flow Diagrams (DFD) provide a graphical representation of the data flow of a system that can be understood by both technical and non-technical users. The models enable software engineers, customers, and users to work together effectively during the analysis and specification of requirements.

A Data Flow Diagram (DFD) visually represents how data moves through a system, showing the inputs, processes, storage, and outputs. It helps stakeholders understand data flow, dependencies, and system interactions without focusing on implementation details.

- **Scope:** Internal data processing of a system
- **Focus:** Flow of data between entities, processes, and data stores
- **Audience:** Business analysts, developers, system architects

Key Components of a DFD

- **External Entities (Sources/Sinks)**
  - Represent external users or systems that **send or receive data** from the system.
  - **Example:** "Customer," "Payment Gateway," "Supplier."
- **Processes**
  - Represent actions that **transform inputs into outputs**.
  - Named using **verb-noun** format (e.g., "Verify Login," "Process Order").

- **Data Stores** 🗁
  - Represent places where **data is stored for later use**.
  - Example: "Customer Database," "Order History."
- **Data Flows** ➡
  - Represent **movement of data** between entities, processes, and data stores.
  - **Example:** "Customer Info," "Payment Details," "Order Confirmation."

Levels of Data Flow Diagrams

Data Flow Diagram (DFD) uses hierarchy to maintain transparency thus multilevel Data Flow Diagram (DFD's) can be created.

1. Level 0 DFD (Context Diagram)

- **High-level overview** of the system.
- Shows **only one main process** and interactions with external entities.

Example: Online Shopping System (Level 0 DFD)

```
+-------------------+
| Customer          | -------> ( Process Order ) -------> | Payment Gateway |
+-------------------+                                     +-----------------+
```

- **External Entities:** Customer, Payment Gateway
- **Main Process:** Process Order
- **Data Flow:** Order details, payment confirmation

2. Level 1 DFD

- Breaks down the main process into sub-processes.
- Shows interactions between different parts of the system.

Example: Online Shopping System (Level 1 DFD)

```
+-------------------+
| Customer          | -----> [1.0 Browse Products] -----> | Product Database |
+-------------------+                                     +-----------------

                   |
                   v
         [2.0 Add to Cart] -----> | Cart Data Store |
                   |
                   v
         [3.0 Place Order] -----> | Order Data Store |
                   |
                   v
         [4.0 Process Payment] -----> | Payment Gateway |
```

Processes

- 1.0 Browse Products
- 2.0 Add to Cart
- 3.0 Place Order
- 4.0 Process Payment

Data Stores

- Product Database
- Cart Data Store
- Order Data Store

External Entities

- Customer, Payment Gateway

Why Use Data Flow Diagrams?

- Clarifies system functionality for all stakeholders.
- Helps identify bottlenecks and inefficiencies in data flow.
- Improves system design before implementation.
- Enhances communication between developers, business analysts, and users.

Comparison of DFD Levels

Level	Purpose	Best For
Level 0 (Context Diagram)	High-level overview, shows system as a single process	"process Order"
Level 1	Breaks down main process into sub-processes	"Browse Products," "Process payment"
Level 2+	More detailed breakdown	"Validate Payment," "Update Order Status"

Example

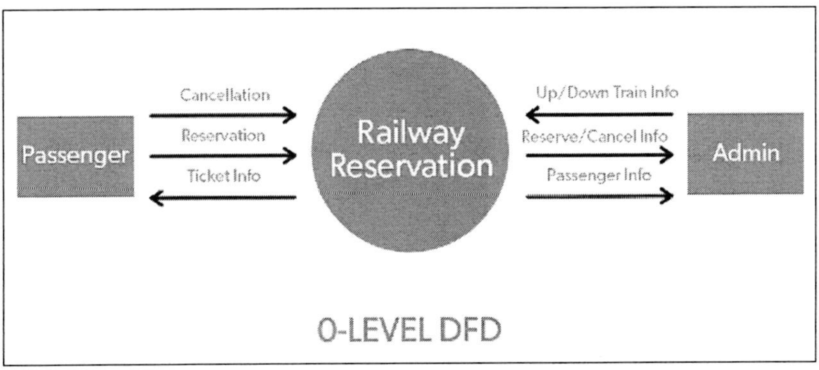

Figure 2.2

Level 0 is the highest-level Data Flow Diagram (DFD), which provides an overview of the entire system. It shows the major processes, data flows, and data stores in the system, without providing any details about the internal workings of these processes.

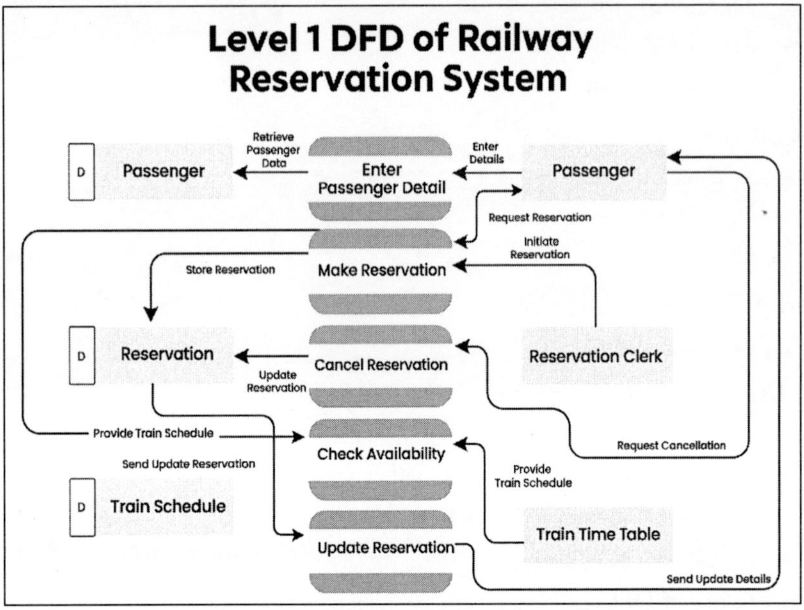

Figure 2.3

1-Level provides a more detailed view of the system by breaking down the major processes identified in the level 0 Data Flow Diagram (DFD) into sub-processes. Each sub-process is depicted as a separate process on the level 1 Data Flow Diagram (DFD). The data flows and data stores associated with each sub-process are also shown.

Advantages of Data Flow Diagram (DFD)

- It helps us to understand the functioning and the limits of a system.
- It is a graphical representation which is very easy to understand as it helps visualize contents.
- Data Flow Diagram represent detailed and well explained diagram of system components.
- It is used as the part of system documentation file.

Disadvantages of Data Flow Diagram (DFD)

- At times Data Flow Diagram (DFD) can confuse the programmers regarding the system.
- Data Flow Diagram takes long time to be generated, and many times due to these reasons analysts are denied permission to work on it.

Data Flow Diagram (DFD) are visual maps that provides a clear understanding of how information moves within an information system. Data Flow Diagrams (DFD) consist of four components i.e. Processes that represent system's functionality, External Entities that represent the end users, data store that represent database or data ware house and data flow that represent how data are flow among these three components.

2.2.2 Entity-Relationship Diagram (ERD) in Requirements Engineering

What Is an Entity-Relationship Diagram (ERD)?

An Entity-Relationship Diagram (ERD) is a visual representation of data and its relationships in a system. It helps in database design and system analysis by showing how different entities interact with each other.

Symbols Used in ER Model

ER Model is used to model the logical view of the system from a data perspective which consists of these symbols:

- **Rectangles:** Rectangles represent Entities in the ER Model.
- **Ellipses:** Ellipses represent Attributes in the ER Model.
- **Diamond:** Diamonds represent Relationships among Entities.
- **Lines:** Lines represent attributes to entities and entity sets with other relationship types.
- **Double Ellipse:** Double Ellipses represent Multi-Valued Attributes.
- **Double Rectangle:** Double Rectangle represents a Weak Entity.

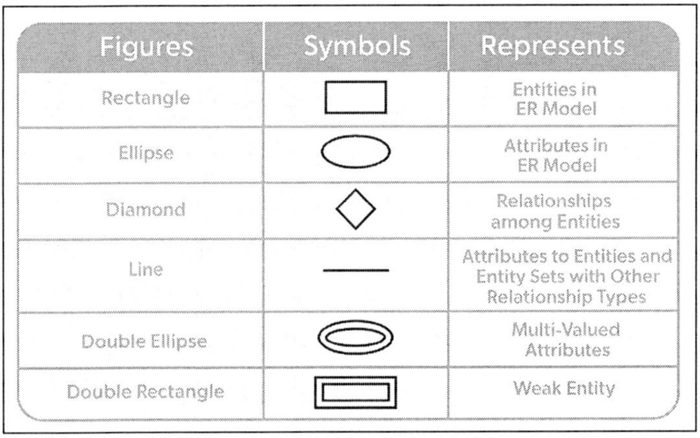

Figure 2.4

Key Components of an ERD

Entities (Tables)

- Represent **real-world objects** in the system.
- Can be **tangible (e.g., Customer, Product)** or **intangible (e.g., Order, Payment)**.
- **Example:** Customer, Order, Product

Attributes (Fields)

- Define **characteristics** of an entity.
- Can be **Primary Keys (PK)** or **Foreign Keys (FK)**.
- **Example:** Customer_ID (PK), Name, Email, Order_ID (PK), Total_Amount

Relationships (Connections)

- Define **how entities are related** to each other.
- Can be **One-to-One (1:1)**, **One-to-Many (1:M)**, or **Many-to-Many (M:N)**.
- **Example:**
  - A **customer places multiple order** → (1:M)
  - An **order contains multiple products** → (M: N)

Example: ERD for an Online Shopping System

Entities & Attributes

Entity	Attributes
Customer	Customer_ID (PK), Name, Email, Address
Order	Order_ID (PK), Date, Customer_ID (FK)
Product	Product_ID(PK), Name, Price
Order_Item	Order_ID (FK), Product_ID (FK), Quantity

ERD Diagram Representation

```
(Customer) 1 ---- (places) ---- * (Order)
(Order) 1 ---- (contains) ---- * (Order_Item) * ---- (Product) 1
```

Relationships

- One Customer can place multiple Orders (1:M)
- One Order can have multiple Products (M: N), resolved using Order_Item table

Types of Relationships in ERD

Relationship Type	Description	Example
One-to-One (1:1)	One entity is related to one other entity	"Each employee has one company ID"
One-to-Many (1:M)	One entity is related to many entities	"One customer can place many orders"
Many-to-Many (M:N)	Many entities relate to many others (requires a junction table)	"An order contains many products, and a product is many orders"

Why Use ERDs?

- Helps in database design by organizing data structure.
- Improves clarity in understanding data relationships.
- Avoids redundancy by normalizing relationships.
- Assists in software development by providing a blueprint for database implementation.

Types of Attributes

1. **Key Attribute**: The attribute which uniquely identifies each entity in the entity set is called the key attribute. For example, Roll_No will be unique for each student. In ER diagram, the key attribute is represented by an oval with underlying lines.

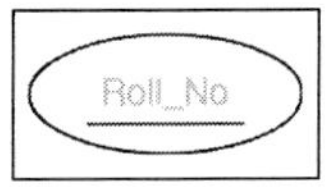

Figure 2.5

2. **Composite Attribute**: An attribute composed of many other attributes is called a composite attribute. For example, the Address attribute of the student Entity type consists of Street, City, State, and Country. In ER diagram, the composite attribute is represented by an oval comprising of ovals.

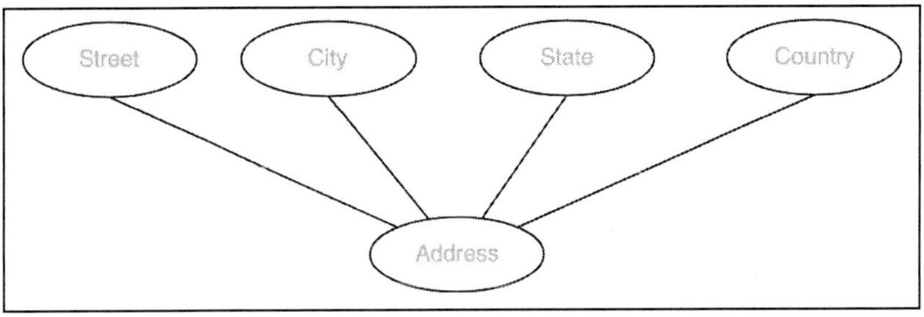

Figure 2.6

3. **Multivalued Attribute:** An attribute consisting of more than one value for a given entity. For example, Phone_No (can be more than one for a given student). In ER diagram, a multivalued attribute is represented by a double oval.
4. **Derived Attribute:** An attribute that can be derived from other attributes of the entity type is known as a derived attribute. e.g.; Age (can be derived from DOB). In ER diagram, the derived attribute is represented by a dashed oval.

   The Complete Entity Type Student with its Attributes can be represented as:

What is Cardinality?

The number of times an entity of an entity set participates in a relationship set is known as cardinality . Cardinality can be of different types:

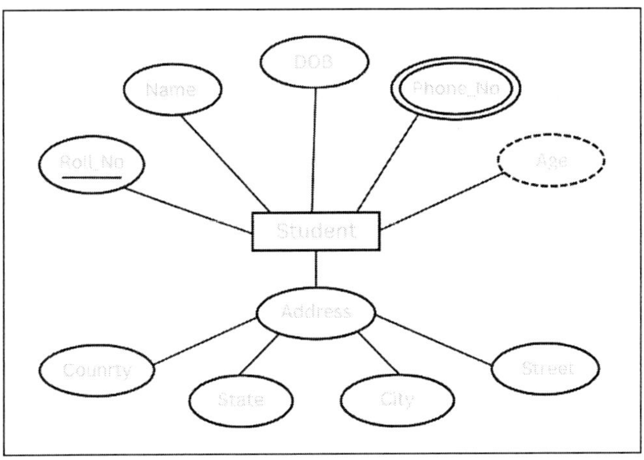

Figure 2.7

1. **One-to-One:** When each entity in each entity set can take part only once in the relationship, the cardinality is one-to-one. Let us assume that a male can marry one female and a female can marry one male. So the relationship will be one-to-one.

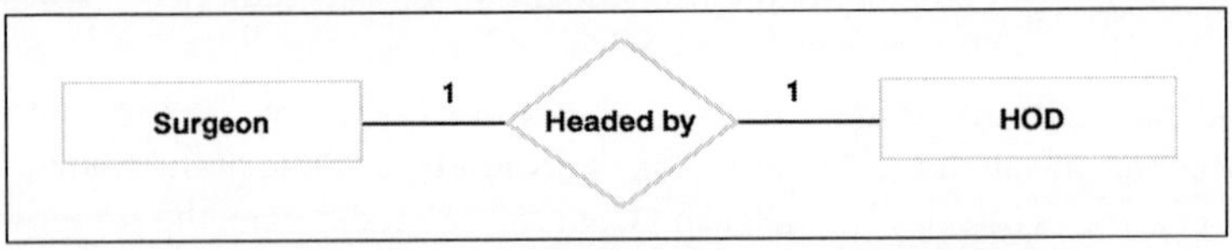

Figure 2.8

2. **One-to-Many:** In one-to-many mapping as well where each entity can be related to more than one entity and the total number of tables that can be used in this is 2. Let us assume that one surgeon department can accommodate many doctors. So the Cardinality will be 1 to M. It means one department has many Doctors.

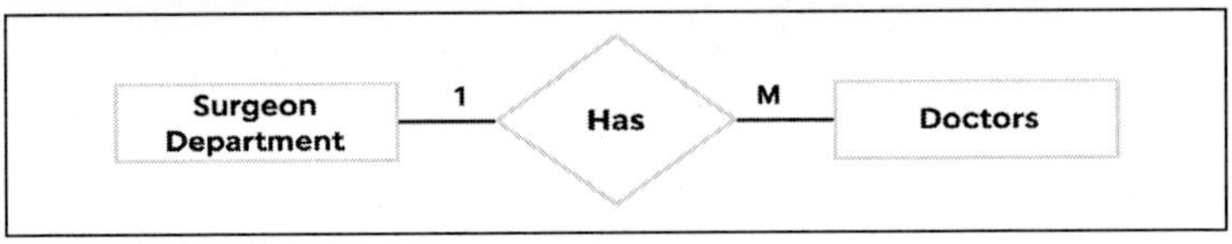

Figure 2.9

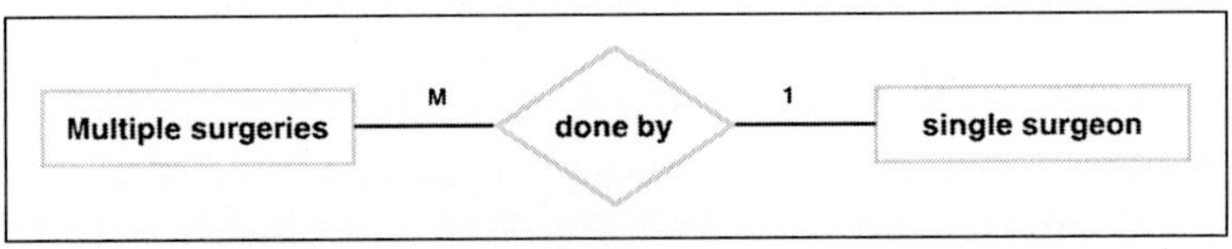

Figure 2.10

3. **Many-to-One:** When entities in one entity set can take part only once in the relationship set and entities in other entity sets can take part more than once in the relationship set, cardinality is many to one. Let us assume that a student can take only one course but one course can be taken by many students. So the cardinality will be n to 1. It means that for one course there can be n students but for one student, there will be only one course.

4. **Many-to-Many:** When entities in all entity sets can take part more than once in the relationship cardinality is many to many. Let us assume that a student can take more than one course and one course can be taken by many students. So the relationship will be many to many.

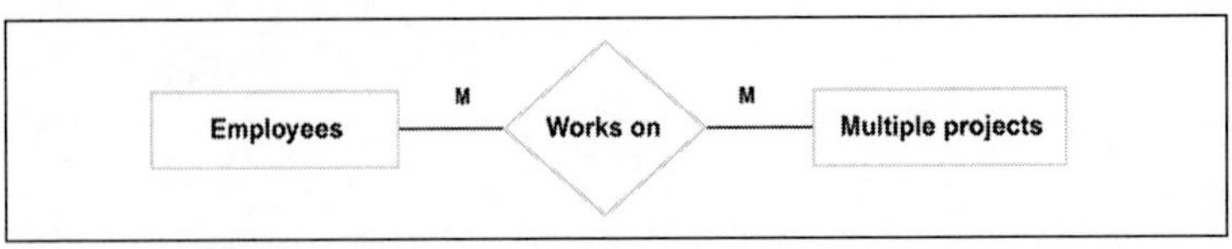

Figure 2.11

An Entity-Relationship (ER) model is a way to visually represent the structure of a database. It shows how different entities (like objects or concepts) are connected and interact with each other through relationships. The model uses diagrams to represent entities as rectangles and relationships as diamonds, making it easier to design and understand databases.

Using Sets, it can be represented as:

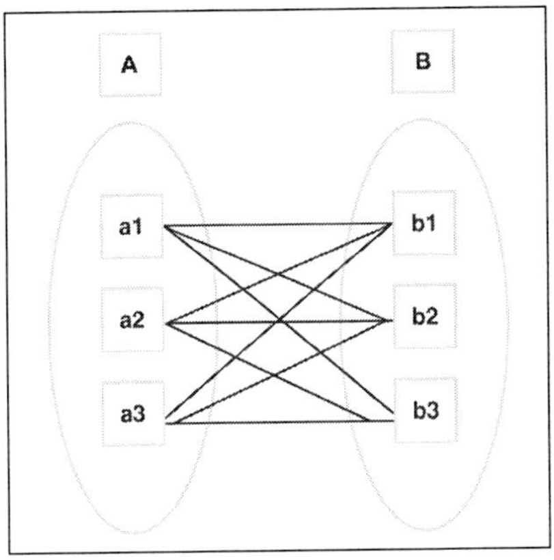

Figure 2.12

2.2.3 Data Dictionary in Requirements Engineering:

What Is a Data Dictionary?

A Data Dictionary is a structured document that defines and describes data elements, their attributes, and relationships in a database or system. It ensures consistency, accuracy, and standardization in data management.

- **Scope:** Defines system data, attributes, and formats
- **Focus:** Data structure, meaning, relationships, and constraints
- **Audience:** Business analysts, database designers, developers

Benefits of a Data Dictionary

- Ensures Data Consistency → Standardizes data usage across systems
- Enhances Data Quality → Avoids duplication and inconsistencies
- Facilitates Communication → Helps developers, analysts, and stakeholders understand Data
- Improves Database Design → Supports normalization and constraint enforcement

Key Components of a Data Dictionary

Attribute	Description
Data Element	Name of the Data field (e.g., Customer_ID, Order_Date)
Data Type	Type of data (e.g., Integer, String, Date)
Size/Length	Maximum allowed characters or digits (e.g., VARCHAAR(50), INT(10))
Description	Purpose and meaning of te field
Default Value	Predefined value (if any)

Attribute	Description
Constraints	Rules applied (e.g., NOT NULL, PRIMARY KEY, FOREIGN KEY)
Relationships	Links to other entities (e.g., FK -> Customer_ID)

- **Data Elements:** This includes the attributes of the data element such as Name, Description, Type, Length, Default Value, and Constraints.
- **Data Structure:** This includes Tables, Fields, Keys, and Indexes.
- **Relationships:** This includes information about the Relationships and Dependencies.
- **Usage and Access Information:** This includes Access Permissions, Usage, and Update Frequency.
- **Data Quality Metrics:** This includes information regarding Accuracy, Completeness, Consistency, and Timelines about data.
- **Data Lineage:** Information about the Source, Transformation, and Destination of data is included.

Example: Data Dictionary for an Online Shopping System:

Data Element	Data Type	Size	Description	Constraints
Customer_ID	INT	10	Unique customer identifier	PRIMARY KEY, NOT NULL
Name	VARCHAR	50	Customer's full name	NOT NULL
Email	VARCHAR	100	Customer email address	UNIQUE, NOT NULL
Order_ID	INT	10	Unique order identifier	PRIMARY KEY, NOT NULL
Order_Date	DATE	-	Data when order was placed	NOT NULL
Product_ID	INT	10	Unique product identifier	FOREIGN KEY -> Products (Products_ID)
Quantity	INT	5	Number of products ordered	CHECK (Quantity > 0)

A data dictionary is an important tool in software engineering for data management. It offers various benefits such as improved consistency, enhanced understanding, better data integration, and many more. However, it comes with some limitations also, such as the need for user training, complexity, scalability issues, and many more. Despite all these challenges, if a data dictionary is effectively managed, it can enhance the overall quality and usability of an organization's data.

2.2.4 State Transition Diagram (STD) in Requirements Engineering

A State Transition Diagram (STD) is a visual representation of how a system, object, or entity moves between different states based on events or conditions. It helps in understanding system behavior, workflow, and decision-making processes.

- **Scope:** System behavior modelling
- **Focus:** Transitions between states due to events
- **Audience:** Business analysts, system architects, developers

Key Components of a State Transition Diagram

- **States** (◍ ◍)
  - Represent different **conditions or situations** of an entity.
  - **Example:** Order Placed, Processing, Shipped, Delivered, Cancelled.
- **Transitions** (➡)
  - Arrows that show **how an entity moves from one state to another**.
  - Example: Order Placed ➡ Processing, Processing ➡ Shipped.
- **Events** (⚡)
  - Triggers that **cause state changes**.
  - **Example:** Payment Received, Shipping Confirmation, Customer Cancellation.
- Initial & Final States (◍ ◍)
  - **Initial state** (◍): Where the process begins.
  - **Final state** (◍): Where the process ends.
  - **Example:** Initial → Order Placed, Final → Delivered or Cancelled.

Example: State Transition Diagram for an Online Shopping Order

States & Transitions:

Initial State: Order Placed

Transitions:

- Order Placed ➡ Processing (Event: Payment Received •)
- Processing ➡ Shipped (Event: Order Packed 📦)
- Shipped ➡ Delivered (Event: Order Received by Customer 📬)
- Processing ➡ Cancelled (Event: Customer Cancelled •)
- **Final States:** Delivered • or Cancelled •

Graphical Representation (Simplified Textual Model)

```
[Order Placed] ●
    |--(Payment Received)--> [Processing]
        |--(Order Packed)--> [Shipped]
            |--(Order Received)--> [Delivered] ●
        |--(Customer Cancelled)--> [Cancelled] ●
```

State Transition Table for Order Processing

Current State	Event	Next State
Order Placed	Payment Received	Processing
Processing	Order Packed	Shipped
Shipped	Order Received by Customer	Delivered
Processing	Customer Cancelled	Cacelled

Why Use a State Transition Diagram?

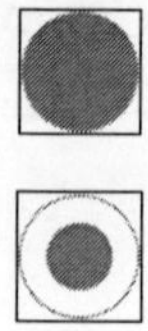

Figure 2.13

- Clarifies system behavior under different conditions.
- Identifies possible errors or bottlenecks in workflow.
- Enhances system design by ensuring smooth transitions.
- Helps in test case design for validating system responses.

Type of State	Description
Initial State	In a System, it represents Starting state.
Final State	In a System, it represents Ending state.
Simple State	In a System, it represents a Simple state with no substructure.
Composite State	In a System, it represents a Composite state with two or more parallel or concurrent states out of which only one state will be active at a time and other states will be inactive.

Now let us see the State Transition Diagram of Automated Teller Machine (ATM) System. In this you will see the processing when the customer performs transactions using ATM card.

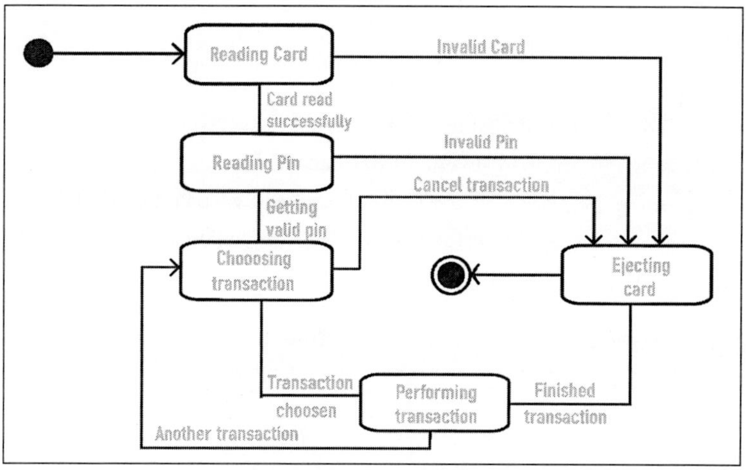

Figure 2.14: *State Transition Diagram for ATM System*

When the customer inserts the bank or credit card in the ATM's card reader, the entry action i.e readcard is performed by the ATM machine. If the card is not valid then the machine will perform exit action. After the card is being read successfully, the ATM machine will ask for Pin. Then the customer enters the pin and ATM machine then reads pin. If the pin entered is not valid then machine will perform exit action. If the pin entered is valid, then the machine further process towards transaction. After successful transaction, machine undergoes the exit action i.e., Reject card that discharges the customer's card.

2.3 Software Requirements Document (SRD)

A Software Requirements Document (SRD) is a detailed specification that outlines the functional and non-functional requirements of a software system. It acts as a formal agreement between stakeholders, including business analysts, developers, testers, and clients, ensuring that all parties have a clear understanding of the project's objectives. The SRD helps in defining the scope, system features, constraints, and expected behavior of the software, reducing ambiguity and ensuring smooth project execution. Below are the key components of an SRD, explained in detail.

1. Introduction

The Introduction section provides an overview of the software system, including its purpose, scope, and objectives. It identifies the stakeholders, such as users, developers, and business owners, and outlines their expectations from the system. This section also describes the intended audience of the document and any background information relevant to the project.

2. System Overview

The System Overview offers a high-level description of the software. It briefly explains what the system does and highlights its main functionalities and components. This section helps stakeholders get a quick understanding of the system's architecture and its role in solving the intended problem.

3. Functional Requirements

Functional Requirements define the core functionalities that the system must provide. These requirements specify what the software should do, including user interactions, data processing, and system outputs. Examples include user authentication, order processing in an e-commerce platform, or report generation in a management system. Each requirement is usually documented using structured statements, often following a format.

4. Non-Functional Requirements

While functional requirements define what the system does, **Non-Functional Requirements** specify how well the system performs. These include performance constraints, security measures, usability, scalability, and system reliability. For example, a non-functional requirement may state:Non-functional requirements are critical for ensuring system efficiency, security, and overall user satisfaction.

5. User Requirements

User Requirements describe how users interact with the system. This section includes user roles, permissions, and use case scenarios that explain different workflows. It defines expected user actions and ensures that the system meets user needs effectively. For instance, in a banking application, different users such as customers and bank administrators may have distinct functionalities.

6. System Requirements

System Requirements define the hardware and software prerequisites for deploying the software. These include operating system compatibility, database requirements, network configurations, and supported platforms. For example, a system requirement might state: "The software must be compatible with Windows, macOS, and Linux operating systems." This section ensures that developers consider infrastructure needs during development.

7. Use Case Scenarios

Use Case Scenarios describe how different types of users interact with the system in real-world scenarios. Each use case includes a step-by-step interaction between the user and the system, covering various functionalities. A simple login use case, for example, would outline how a user enters their credentials, submits them, and receives either access or an error message.

8. Data Flow Diagrams (DFD) & Entity-Relationship Diagram (ERD)

To visualize how data moves within the system, **Data Flow Diagrams (DFDs)** and **Entity-Relationship Diagrams (ERDs)** are included. DFDs represent how data is processed within the system, showing inputs, processes, and outputs. ERDs illustrate database structure, showing relationships between different data entities. These diagrams are essential for developers to design and implement the system correctly.

9. Assumptions & Constraints

This section lists any **assumptions and constraints** that impact system development. Assumptions include conditions expected to be true, such as users having stable internet access. Constraints include technological or business limitations, such as budget constraints or regulatory requirements. For example: "The system will be accessible only via web browsers and will not have a mobile application in the initial release."

10. Appendices & References

The final section includes **Appendices & References**, which provide additional resources, supporting documents, and references used in drafting the SRD. This may include links to industry standards, technical documents, or previous project reports.

A Software Requirements Document is an essential blueprint that defines the scope, functionalities, and constraints of a software system. It ensures that all stakeholders have a shared understanding of the system before development begins. By clearly documenting requirements, an SRD helps in reducing misunderstandings, improving project management, and ensuring a smooth development process.

2.4 Requirement Engineering Process

The Requirement Engineering Process is a systematic approach to gathering, analyzing, documenting, and validating the requirements of a software system. It ensures that the final product meets the needs of stakeholders while maintaining feasibility and efficiency. This process is crucial for reducing errors, improving software quality, and preventing project failures due to unclear or incomplete requirements.

- Feasibility studies
- Requirements elicitation and Analysis

2.4.1 Feasibility studies

A Feasibility Study is a crucial step in the Requirement Engineering Process, conducted before defining the final requirements of a software system. It evaluates whether the proposed system is practical, cost-effective, and technically possible within existing constraints. The goal is to determine if the project should proceed and identify potential risks early.

Feasibility Study in the Requirement Engineering Process

The **Requirement Engineering Process** consists of the following stages:

- Requirement Elicitation (Gathering Requirements)
- Requirement Analysis & Negotiation
- Feasibility Study
- Requirement Specification (SRS Documentation)
- Requirement Validation
- Requirement Management & Change Control

The Feasibility Study occurs after gathering and analyzing requirements but before finalizing the Software Requirements Specification (SRS). If the study determines the project is infeasible, requirements may need to be revised, or the project may be re-evaluated.

Key Aspects of Feasibility Studies in Requirement Engineering

1. Technical Feasibility

- Evaluates whether the required technology, software, and hardware exist to develop the system.
- Checks compatibility with current infrastructure.
- Identifies technical risks and solutions.
- **Example:** Can AI-driven medical diagnosis software work with existing hospital IT systems?

2. Economic Feasibility (Cost-Benefit Analysis)

- Assesses whether the project is financially viable.
- Compares the estimated **development, maintenance, and operational costs** with the expected **benefits and revenue**.
- **Example:** Will an e-commerce platform generate enough revenue to justify its cost?

3. Operational Feasibility

- Examines if the software meets user needs and integrates smoothly into business operations.
- Evaluates user acceptance and training requirements.
- **Example:** Will employees be able to switch from a manual inventory system to an automated one?

4. Schedule Feasibility (Time Feasibility)

- Determines whether the project can be completed within the required timeframe.
- Identifies risks of **delays** and **bottlenecks** in development.
- **Example:** Can a ride-hailing app be developed within 6 months for a competitive launch?

5. Legal & Regulatory Feasibility

- Ensures the software complies with laws, industry standards, and regulations.
- Checks **data privacy laws (e.g., GDPR, HIPAA)** and cybersecurity requirements.
- **Example:** Does a financial software system comply with banking regulations?

How Feasibility Studies Influence Requirements Engineering

- If the feasibility study shows positive results, the requirements are finalized and documented in the SRS.
- If issues are found, the requirements may need modifications to ensure feasibility.
- If the project is deemed infeasible, alternative solutions or technologies may be explored.

Outcome of Feasibility Study in Requirement Engineering

- A Feasibility Report summarizing findings.
- A decision on whether to proceed, modify, or abandon the project.
- A list of project risks and mitigation strategies.

2.4.2 Requirements Elicitation and Analysis

1. Requirements Elicitation

What is Requirements Elicitation?

Requirements elicitation is the process of gathering information from stakeholders to determine what they need from a software system. It is the first step in the Requirement Engineering Process, ensuring that the system meets business goals and user expectations.

Techniques for Requirements Elicitation

1. Interviews

- One-on-one or group discussions with stakeholders to collect requirements.
- Can be structured (predefined questions) or unstructured (open-ended).
- **Example:** Interviewing customers to understand features needed in an e-commerce app.

2. Surveys & Questionnaires

- Collecting structured feedback from a large number of users.
- Helps in identifying common patterns and needs.
- **Example:** Sending a questionnaire to employees for feedback on HR software improvements.

3. Observation

- Watching users interact with an existing system to understand workflow and pain points.

- Useful when stakeholders find it difficult to express their needs explicitly.
- **Example:** Observing how a cashier handles transactions in a supermarket to automate the process.

4. Workshops & Brainstorming

- Collaborative sessions to gather and refine requirements with multiple stakeholders.
- Helps resolve conflicts and generate creative ideas.
- **Example:** Organizing a brainstorming session with doctors and nurses to define hospital management software features.

5. Prototyping

- Creating a basic model of the system (wireframes, mockups) to gather early feedback.
- Helps stakeholders visualize the system before full development.
- **Example:** Developing a prototype for an online banking portal before coding begins.

Key Objectives of Requirements Elicitation

- Identify stakeholder needs and expectations.
- Define functional and non-functional requirements.
- Resolve conflicts between different stakeholders.
- Ensure feasibility and practicality of requirements.

2. Requirements Analysis

What is Requirements Analysis?

Requirements analysis is the process of refining, prioritizing, and validating the gathered requirements to ensure they are complete, clear, and feasible.

Steps in Requirements Analysis

1. Classifying Requirements

- **Functional Requirements:** Define what the system must do (e.g., "Users should be able to log in").
- **Non-Functional Requirements:** Define system performance, security, usability, etc. (e.g., "The system must support 1,000 users simultaneously").

2. Checking for Completeness & Consistency

- Ensuring that all business needs are covered without contradictions.
- **Example:** Checking if a banking app includes both fund transfers and transaction history features.

3. Prioritization of Requirements

- Assigning importance to requirements based on business impact and feasibility.
- **Example:** Implementing a "Buy Now" button in an e-commerce site before adding a wishlist feature.

4. Modeling Requirements

- **Use Case Modeling:** Defines interactions between users and the system.
- **Data Flow Diagrams (DFD):** Shows how data moves within the system.
- **Entity-Relationship Diagrams (ERD):** Describes the database structure.

5. Conflict Resolution

- Addressing disagreements among stakeholders regarding system features.
- **Example:** Balancing security features required by IT with ease of use demanded by customers.

Key Objectives of Requirements Analysis

- Ensure that requirements are unambiguous, complete, and consistent.
- Prioritize requirements based on business value and feasibility.
- Identify and resolve conflicting requirements from different stakeholders.
- Define requirements in a structured format like use cases, data flow diagrams (DFDs), and entity-relationship diagrams (ERDs).

Challenges in Requirements Elicitation and Analysis

- **Incomplete or vague requirements:** Users may not fully understand their own needs.
- **Conflicting requirements:** Different stakeholders may have different priorities.
- **Changing requirements:** Business needs and technology evolve over time.
- **Communication barriers:** Misunderstandings between technical and non-technical stakeholders.

Outcome of Requirements Elicitation and Analysis

- A refined Software Requirements Specification (SRS) document.
- Defined use cases, data models, and workflows.
- Validated and prioritized list of functional & non-functional requirements.
- Approved scope for development to minimize project risks.

2.5 Requirements Validation

What is Requirements Validation?

Requirements Validation is the process of ensuring that the gathered and analyzed requirements correctly define the system to be developed. It ensures that the requirements are complete, consistent, feasible, and aligned with business needs before proceeding to development.

Techniques for Requirements Validation

1. Requirements Reviews

- Conduct formal or informal meetings with stakeholders to review requirements.
- Helps identify missing, incorrect, or conflicting requirements.
- **Example:** A **business analyst, developer, and end-user** review the requirements of a payroll management system.

2. Prototyping

- Developing a **mock-up or prototype** to allow stakeholders to visualize the system before actual development.
- Helps validate **user interface (UI), workflow, and expected functionality**.
- **Example:** A prototype of an e-commerce website's checkout process is tested by customers.

3. Model Validation

- Using diagrams such as **Use Case Diagrams, Data Flow Diagrams (DFD), and Entity-Relationship Diagrams (ERD)** to validate relationships and workflows.
- Ensures logical consistency in the system.
- **Example:** A banking system's DFD is validated to check how data flows between customers and accounts.

4. Test Case Generation

- Writing test cases based on requirements to check if they can be **realistically implemented and tested**.
- Ensures that the requirements are **verifiable**.
- **Example:** A test case for a **login system** checks if the software correctly validates usernames and passwords.

5. Consistency & Completeness Checks

- Ensures that **there are no conflicting or missing requirements**.
- **Example:** If a system has a "password reset" feature but no "email verification" requirement, it's flagged as incomplete.

6. Stakeholder Validation & Approval

- Involves **clients, end-users, and project managers** in reviewing and approving requirements.
- Ensures that all expectations are met before moving forward.
- **Example:** A hospital management system's requirements are reviewed and signed off by doctors and nurses.

Objectives of Requirements Validation

- Verify that the requirements accurately represent stakeholder needs.

- Ensure that requirements are complete, consistent, and unambiguous.
- Identify and correct any errors, conflicts, or unrealistic expectations.
- Reduce future development costs by catching issues early.
- Confirm that requirements align with legal, security, and business constraints.

Challenges in Requirements Validation

- **Ambiguous Requirements:** Vague or unclear requirements can cause misinterpretation.
- **Conflicting Requirements:** Different stakeholders may have different expectations.
- **Overlooked Requirements:** Critical functionalities may be missed.
- **Stakeholder Availability:** Difficulty in gathering timely feedback from key decision-makers.

Outcome of Requirements Validation

- A validated Software Requirements Specification (SRS) document.
- Elimination of errors, inconsistencies, and ambiguities before development.
- Reduced development costs due to early issue identification.
- Approval from stakeholders to proceed with system design and development.

2.6 Requirements Management

What is Requirements Management?

Requirements Management is the process of documenting, tracking, and controlling software requirements throughout the project lifecycle. It ensures that changes to requirements are managed systematically, avoiding scope creep and misalignment with business goals.

Key Activities in Requirements Management

1. Requirements Documentation

- Creating a **Software Requirements Specification (SRS)** document.
- Ensuring all requirements are **clearly defined, categorized, and prioritized**.
- **Example:** Recording functional and non-functional requirements for an **inventory management system**.

2. Requirements Traceability

- Establishing links between requirements and **design, development, and testing**.
- Helps track **changes and their impact** on other parts of the system.
- **Example:** Using a **traceability matrix** to connect user authentication requirements with security test cases.

3. Requirements Prioritization

- Ranking requirements based on **business value, feasibility, and urgency**.
- Helps in managing scope when there are budget or time constraints.
- **Example:** Prioritizing **"Secure Payment Processing"** over **"Wishlist Feature"** in an e-commerce application.

4. Change Management

- Handling modifications in requirements **without disrupting the project**.
- Includes **impact analysis, stakeholder approval, and documentation updates**.
- **Example:** If a bank wants **biometric login** instead of password authentication, a change request process is followed.

5. Requirements Version Control

- Maintaining different versions of requirements to track changes over time.
- **Example:** Using **Requirement Management Tools** like Jira, IBM DOORS, or Trello to track modifications.

6. Requirements Validation & Verification

- Ensuring that requirements remain **consistent, testable, and achievable** throughout development.
- **Example:** Running validation sessions to ensure new updates comply with **security regulations**.

Challenges in Requirements Management

- **Frequent Requirement Changes:** Uncontrolled modifications can delay projects.
- **Poor Documentation:** Unclear or missing requirements lead to misunderstandings.
- **Lack of Stakeholder Involvement:** Misalignment between user needs and the final product.
- **Traceability Issues:** Difficulty in tracking how requirements evolve over time.

Outcome of Effective Requirements Management

- Well-documented, clear, and traceable requirements.
- Fewer errors and conflicts in later stages of development.
- Improved project efficiency and reduced costs due to better change management.
- Higher customer satisfaction as the system meets business and user needs.

Objectives of Requirements Management

- Maintain a clear, organized repository of all requirements.
- Ensure traceability from initial elicitation to final implementation.
- Manage requirement changes efficiently while minimizing project risks.
- Ensure alignment with stakeholder needs, business goals, and compliance standards
- Facilitate effective communication among developers, analysts, and stakeholders.

This page is intentionally left blank!

3 UNIT

SOFTWARE DESIGNS

3.1 Design Process and Concepts

The Software Design Process is a systematic approach to transforming requirements into a structured system. It starts with requirement analysis to define functional and non-functional needs, followed by high-level design, where the system's architecture is planned. Then, low-level design focuses on defining modules, data structures, and algorithms for implementation. The system is then developed, tested, and validated to ensure functionality and performance. Finally, it is deployed and maintained, with continuous monitoring and updates for improvements.

Stages of the Software Design Process

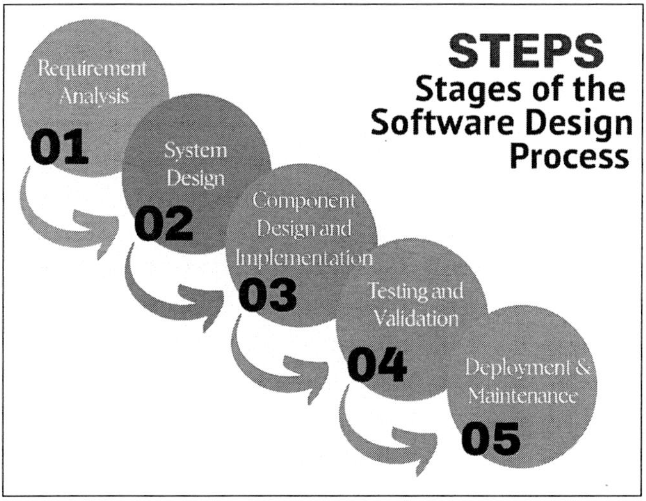

Figure 3.1

Requirement Analysis

- Understand and document functional (what the system should do) and non-functional (performance, security, scalability) requirements.
- Identify system constraints and dependencies.

Example: For an e-commerce system, functional requirements include "users can add items to a cart," while non-functional requirements may specify "the system should handle 10,000 concurrent users."

System Design

- Defines the system's overall structure and communication between components.
- Choose an appropriate architecture based on requirements (e.g., Layered Architecture, Client-Server, Microservices).
- Identify major system components (e.g., databases, services, APIs, UI components).

Example: A banking system may adopt a Layered Architecture with Presentation, Business Logic, and Database layers.

Component Design (Low-Level Design / Detailed Design)

- Define the internal structure of each module.
- Identify data structures, algorithms, class hierarchies, and interfaces.
- Ensure modularity, reusability, and maintainability.

Example: In Object-Oriented Design (OOD), a "User" class may have attributes like name, email, password and methods like login() and logout().

Implementation

- Convert the design into actual code.
- Follow best practices like coding standards, design patterns, and version control.
- Conduct code reviews and static analysis.

Example: In a Java-based project, different teams implement backend services and frontend components separately.

Testing and Validation

- Ensure the software works as expected through multiple levels of testing:
  - Unit Testing (Testing individual modules)
  - Integration Testing (Ensuring modules work together)
  - System Testing (End-to-end validation)
  - User Acceptance Testing (UAT) (Final user approval)

Example: A mobile app undergoes UAT to ensure it meets user expectations before launch.

Deployment & Maintenance

Deployment & Maintenance are the final stages of the software development lifecycle, ensuring that the software is successfully released and remains functional over time.

- Deploy the software in staging (test environment) before going live in production.
- Continuously monitor and update the system to fix bugs and improve performance.
- Implement scalability improvements based on user feedback.

Example: A SaaS platform may receive regular feature updates and security patches.

Principles of Good Software Design

- **Modularity:** Break down the system into smaller, reusable components.
- **Encapsulation:** Hide internal details and expose only necessary functionality.
- **Low Coupling & High Cohesion:** Minimize dependencies and maximize self-contained functionality.

- **Scalability:** The system should handle increased load efficiently.
- **Maintainability:** The design should support easy modifications.

The software design process ensures that a system is **well-structured, efficient, and scalable.** A well-planned design reduces development time, minimizes risks, and enhances system quality.

Software Design Concepts

Software design concepts provide the foundation for creating efficient, maintainable, and scalable software systems. These concepts guide developers in structuring software solutions that meet business requirements while ensuring reliability and performance.

1. Abstraction

Abstraction simplifies complex systems by hiding unnecessary details and exposing only essential features. For example, a **sorting function** abstracts the underlying algorithm, allowing users to sort data without knowing the implementation details.

2. Modularity

Modularity divides a system into smaller, **independent** modules that can be developed, tested, and maintained separately. Each module handles a specific function, improving code **reusability, maintainability, and scalability**.

3. Encapsulation

Encapsulation restricts direct access to an object's internal details, ensuring that data is **protected and manipulated only through well-defined interfaces**. This concept enhances **security and integrity** in object-oriented programming.

4. Coupling and Cohesion

- **Low Coupling:** Modules should have minimal dependencies on each other, making them more independent and easier to modify.
- **High Cohesion:** A module should focus on a single, well-defined task, ensuring better readability and maintainability.

5. Separation of Concerns (SoC)

Different aspects of a system should be handled separately. For example, **in the MVC (Model-View-Controller) architecture**, the model manages data, the view handles the UI, and the controller processes user inputs.

These core software design concepts ensure that systems are efficient, adaptable, and robust, reducing complexity and improving long-term development success.

3.2 Popular Software Design Methods

Different software design methods help structure and organize system development based on project requirements and complexity. Below are some widely used design approaches.

- Modular Decomposition
- Event oriented
- Object-oriented design

3.2.1 Modular Decomposition

Module decomposition is a critical aspect of system design, enabling the breakdown of complex systems into smaller, more manageable modules or components. These modules encapsulate specific functionalities, making the system easier to understand, maintain, and scale. In this article, we will explore the concept of module decomposition in system design, its benefits, common techniques, and best practices.

What is Module Decomposition?

Module decomposition is a process in system design and architecture where a complex system is broken down into smaller, more manageable modules or components. Each module encapsulates a specific functionality, data, or behavior of the system, and modules are designed to interact with each other through well-defined interfaces.

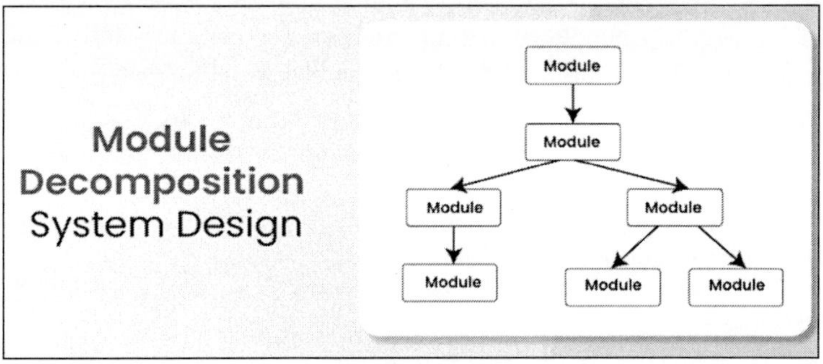

Figure 3.2

Importance of Module Decomposition in System Design

- **Understanding**: Increases comprehension of the system by dissecting it into more manageable, smaller components.
- **Maintainability**: Isolating modifications to particular modules makes maintenance and upgrades easier.
- **Reusability**: Encourages the reuse of modules within the same project or between separate projects.
- **Scalability**: Divides larger, more complex systems into smaller, easier-to-manage pieces, enabling more efficient scaling.
- **Testing**: Isolates modules to make the process of testing and debugging easier.

Principles and Objectives of Module Decomposition

- **Coupling**: To reduce the impact of changes, modules should have low coupling, which means they should be largely independent of one another or loosely connected.
- **Scalability**: Modules have to be created with future expansion and requirement modifications in mind.
- **Information Hiding**: Only the interfaces required to communicate with other modules should be exposed by modules, which should encapsulate their internal workings.

- **Cohesiveness**: A module should have a high level of cohesiveness if its components are closely tied to one another and concentrated on a particular duty or task.
- **Reusability**: To cut down on duplication and increase productivity, modules ought to be made so they can be used again in various situations.

Role of Module Decomposition in System Architecture

Module decomposition, which arranges a system's components and their interactions, is essential for designing a system's architecture. It aids in the system's structural organization to promote effective growth, upkeep, and evolution.

- **Modularity**:
  - Module decomposition helps break down a complex system into smaller, more manageable modules.
  - Each module can be developed, tested, and maintained independently, making the overall system easier to understand and modify.
- **Encapsulation**:
  - Modules encapsulate related functionality, data, and behavior, hiding the internal details from other modules.
  - This reduces dependencies and helps ensure that changes to one module do not affect other modules.
- **Abstraction**:
  - Modules provide a level of abstraction, allowing developers to focus on the interface and functionality of each module without needing to understand its internal implementation.
  - This simplifies the design and improves maintainability.

Overall, module decomposition is essential in system architecture for creating systems that are flexible, maintainable, and scalable. It provides a structured approach to designing complex systems, making them easier to develop, understand, and maintain over time.

3.2.2 Event Oriented

Event-oriented design, particularly within the context of event-driven architecture (EDA), has several key characteristics that define its approach to software engineering.

Core Characteristics

- **Asynchronous Communication:**
  - A fundamental aspect is that components communicate through events without requiring immediate responses. This decoupling allows for greater flexibility and responsiveness.
- **Loose Coupling:**
  - Components are designed to be independent, interacting through the exchange of events. This minimizes dependencies and makes systems more adaptable to change.
- **Real-time Responsiveness:**
  - EDA enables systems to react to events as they occur, facilitating real-time processing and immediate responses. This is crucial for applications that require timely updates.

- **Scalability:**
  - The decoupled nature of EDA allows for individual components to be scaled independently, making it easier to handle increased workloads.
- **Event-Driven Flow:**
  - The system's behavior is driven by the occurrence of events. The flow of control is determined by the events that are generated and consumed.

Event-oriented design, particularly within the context of event-driven architecture (EDA), has several key characteristics that define its approach to software engineering. Here's a breakdown:

Core Characteristics

- **Asynchronous Communication:**
  - A fundamental aspect is that components communicate through events without requiring immediate responses. This decoupling allows for greater flexibility and responsiveness.
- **Loose Coupling:**
  - Components are designed to be independent, interacting through the exchange of events. This minimizes dependencies and makes systems more adaptable to change.
- **Real-time Responsiveness:**
  - EDA enables systems to react to events as they occur, facilitating real-time processing and immediate responses. This is crucial for applications that require timely updates.
- **Scalability:**
  - The decoupled nature of EDA allows for individual components to be scaled independently, making it easier to handle increased workloads.
- **Event-Driven Flow:**
  - The system's behavior is driven by the occurrence of events. The flow of control is determined by the events that are generated and consumed.
- **Event Producers and Consumers:**
  - The architecture typically involves event producers that generate events and event consumers that process those events.
- **Event Routers/Brokers:**
  - These components facilitate the distribution of events from producers to consumers, often providing features like filtering and routing.
- **Fault Tolerance:**
  - By logging and storing events, EDA can enhance system reliability and enable recovery from failures.
- **Flexibility and Agility:**
  - Because of the loose coupling, and the way that new consumers of event data can be added without effecting producers, EDA allows for systems to be more flexible, and agile in the face of changing requirements.

Key Concepts

- **Events:**
  - Represent a change in state or a significant occurrence within the system.
- **Event Streams:**
  - Sequences of events that can be processed in real-time.
- **Publish/Subscribe:**
  - A common pattern where producers publish events to a channel, and consumers subscribe to those channels to receive events.

In essence, event-oriented design promotes a reactive and adaptable approach to software development, enabling systems to respond effectively to dynamic environments.

Example: Event-Oriented Design in JavaScript (GUI Event Handling)

- The button **listens** for a "click" event and executes a **handler function** when clicked.

```
document.getElementById("btn").addEventListener("click", function() {
    alert("Button Clicked! Event Triggered.");
});
```

- **Key Takeaway:** Event-oriented design is ideal for **asynchronous, real-time, and interactive systems**. It enhances **modularity, flexibility, and scalability** but requires careful event management to avoid complexity.

3.2.3 Object-Oriented Design (OOD) – System Design

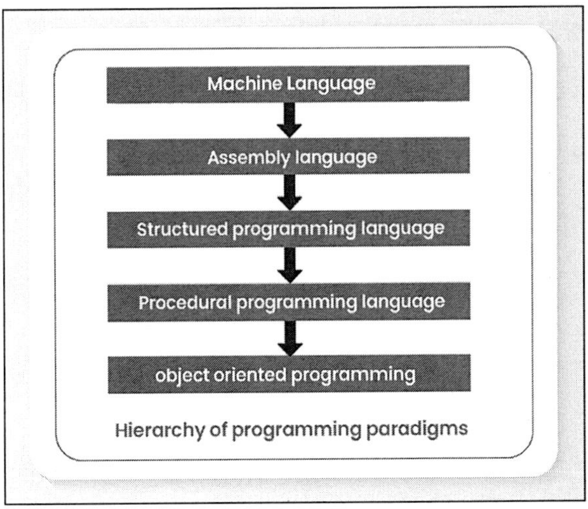

Figure 3.3

A crucial method for system design is object-oriented design (OOD), which places an intense focus on scalability, modularity, and reusability. OOD resembles real-world systems by encapsulating data and behavior into objects, which facilitates understanding programs and maintenance. By utilizing concepts like inheritance, polymorphism, and encapsulation, this approach promotes resilient and adaptable architectures.

What is Object-Oriented Design (OOD)?

Object-oriented design (OOD) is a programming technique that solves software problems by building a system of interrelated objects. It makes use of the concepts of classes and objects, encapsulation, inheritance, and polymorphism to model real-world entities and their interactions. A system architecture that is modular, adaptable, and simple to understand and maintain is produced using OOD.

Design

Object-Oriented Design (OOD) is important in system design due to several key reasons:

- **Modularity**: OOD simplifies development and maintenance by decomposing complicated structures into smaller, more manageable components.
- **Reusability**: Objects and classes can be reused across different projects, reducing redundancy and saving time.
- **Scalability**: OOD facilitates system growth by making it simple to incorporate new objects without interfering with already-existing functionality.
- **Maintainability**: Encapsulation of data and behavior within objects simplifies troubleshooting and updates, enhancing system reliability.
- **Clear Mapping to Real-World Problems**: By modeling software after real-world entities and their interactions, OOD makes systems more intuitive and easier to understand.
- **Flexibility and Extensibility**: Through inheritance and polymorphism, OOD allows for extending and adapting systems with minimal changes, accommodating future requirements efficiently.

Key Principles of OOD

A number of fundamental principles support object-oriented design (OOD), helping in the development of reliable, expandable, and maintainable systems:

- **Encapsulation**: Bundling data with methods that operate on the data, restricting direct access to some components and protecting object integrity.
- **Abstraction**: Simplifying complex systems by modeling classes appropriate to the problem domain, highlighting essential features while hiding unnecessary details.
- **Inheritance**: Establishing a hierarchy between classes, allowing derived classes to inherit properties and behaviors from base classes, promoting code reuse and extension.
- **Polymorphism**: Enabling objects to be treated as instances of their parent class, allowing one interface to be used for a general class of actions, improving flexibility and integration.
- **Composition**: Building complex objects by combining simpler ones, promoting reuse and flexible designs.

SOLID Principles

- **Single Responsibility Principle (SRP)**: A class should have one, and only one, reason to change.
- **Open/Closed Principle (OCP)**: Classes should be open for extension but closed for modification.

- **Liskov Substitution Principle (LSP)**: Subtypes must be substitutable for their base types without altering the correctness of the program.
- **Interface Segregation Principle (ISP)**: Clients should not be forced to depend on interfaces they do not use.
- **Dependency Inversion Principle (DIP)**: High-level modules should not depend on low-level modules. Both should depend on abstractions.

Design Patterns in Object-Oriented Design (OOD)

Design patterns in Object-Oriented Design (OOD) are proven solutions to common problems that arise in software design. These patterns provide templates that help to structure code in an efficient and maintainable way. Here are some of the most commonly used design patterns in OOD:

- **Creational Patterns:** Creational patterns deal with object creation mechanisms, trying to create objects in a manner suitable to the situation. Some key creational patterns include:
- **Singleton**: Ensures a class has only one instance and provides a global point of access to it.
- **Factory Method**: Defines an interface for creating an object, but lets subclasses alter the type of objects that will be created.
- **Structural Patterns**: Structural patterns deal with object composition or structure, ensuring that if one part changes, the entire structure does not need to do so. Some key structural patterns include:
- **Adapter**: Converts the interface of a class into another interface the clients expect. It lets classes work together that couldn't otherwise because of incompatible interfaces.
- **Composite**: Composes objects into tree structures to represent part-whole hierarchies. It lets clients treat individual objects and compositions of objects uniformly.

UML Diagrams for Visualizing OOD

Diagrams created using the Unified Modeling Language (UML) are useful tools for understanding and clarifying object-oriented system structure. They serve as a blueprint, showing the interactions between many components of a system, which makes difficult concepts simpler to understand and communicate.

Here are some common UML diagrams and how they contribute to object-oriented design:

- **Class Diagrams**: These diagrams show the structure of a system by highlighting the classes, their attributes, and relationships. This is useful in visualizing how data and behaviors are organized, which is the foundation of object-oriented design.
- **Sequence Diagrams**: Sequence diagrams illustrate how objects in a system interact over time. They show the flow of messages and actions, helping designers see the order in which things happen. This makes it easier to understand the dynamic behavior of a system.
- **State Diagrams**: State diagrams represent the various states of an object and the transitions between them. They help designers understand how objects respond to different events, which is key for designing systems that change over time.

Example

```
class Customer {
    String name;
    String email;

    void placeOrder() {
        System.out.println("Order placed!");
    }
}
```

By using these diagrams, developers can make sure everyone has a clear picture of the system's structure and behavior, making it easier to collaborate and avoid misunderstandings.

3.3 Transition from Analysis to Design

A crucial stage in the software development life cycle (SDLC) is the shift from analysis to design, where the requirements and system models created during analysis are transformed into a tangible system design. This stage fills in the gaps between the requirements (what the system must do) and the design (how it will accomplish those goals).

Steps in Transition from Analysis to Design

Step 1: Reviewing System Requirements

Output from Analysis

- Functional and non-functional requirements.
- System constraints and business rules.
- Use case diagrams and system models.

Key Considerations for Design

- Performance, scalability, and security requirements.
- User interface (UI) needs.
- System interactions with external entities (APIs, databases, etc.).

Step 2: Identifying System Components & Architecture

Convert high-level models into modular components

- Define system **architecture** (Layered, Microservices, Client-Server, etc.).
- Identify key **modules** and their **responsibilities**.
- Establish relationships between modules using **component diagrams**.

Example: E-Commerce System

- User Management Module
- Product Catalog Module
- Shopping Cart Module

- Order Processing Module
- Payment Gateway Module

Step 3: Defining Data Structures and Flow

Convert Data Models into Database Design

- Use **ER diagrams** to design tables and relationships.
- Ensure **data normalization** and integrity.

Refine Data Flow

- Convert **Data Flow Diagrams (DFD)** into detailed **flowcharts**.
- Define how data moves **between modules**.

Step 4: Creating Software Design Models

From Logical Models to Physical Design

- Transform **use case diagrams** into **class diagrams** (if using OOP).
- Create **sequence diagrams** to define interactions.
- Design **UI wireframes** to guide front-end development.

Example: A Banking App Transition

- Use Case: "User transfers funds"
- Design Output:
  - **Class Diagram:** Defines objects (Account, Transaction, User).
  - **Sequence Diagram:** Shows steps from user request to transaction completion.
  - **UI Mock-up:** Screens for entering account details and confirming transfer.

Step 5: Establishing Design Constraints & Standards

Ensure feasibility of design based on

- Performance requirements (e.g., response time < 2 sec).
- Security (e.g., encryption for sensitive data).
- Maintainability (e.g., modular structure, coding standards).

Define Development Standards

- Programming languages and frameworks.
- Version control strategy (e.g., Git workflows).
- Documentation and testing procedures.

Step 6: Validating and Refining the Design

Evaluate Design Feasibility

- Review with stakeholders (business, development, testing teams).
- Perform **prototyping** to validate UI and interactions.
- Identify potential **risks and optimizations**.

Output from Design Phase

- System architecture diagrams.
- Database schema.
- Component specifications.
- UI wireframes.
- Security & performance guidelines

The transition from analysis to design ensures that business requirements are successfully translated into a well-structured system blueprint. A good design lays the foundation for efficient development, scalability, and maintainability.

3.4 Architectural Design

The software needs an architectural design to represent the design of the software. IEEE defines architectural design as "the process of defining a collection of hardware and software components and their interfaces to establish the framework for the development of a computer system." The software that is built for computer-based systems can exhibit one of these many architectural styles.

System Category Consists of

- A set of components(eg: a database, computational modules) that will perform a function required by the system.
- The set of connectors will help in coordination, communication, and cooperation between the components.
- Conditions that define how components can be integrated to form the system.
- Semantic models that help the designer to understand the overall properties of the system.

Taxonomy of Architectural Styles

1. Data centered Architectures

- A data store will reside at the center of this architecture and is accessed frequently by the other components that update, add, delete, or modify the data present within the store.
- The figure illustrates a typical data-centered style. The client software accesses a central repository. Variations of this approach are used to transform the repository into a blackboard when data related to the client or data of interest for the client change the notifications to client software.

2. Data flow Architectures

- This kind of architecture is used when input data is transformed into output data through a series of computational manipulative components.
- The figure represents pipe-and-filter architecture since it uses both pipe and filter and it has a set of components called filters connected by lines.

  Pipes are used to transmitting data from one component to the next.

3. Call and Return Architectures

It is used to create a program that is easy to scale and modify. Many sub-styles exist within this category. Two of them are explained below.

1. **Remote procedure call architecture:** This components is used to present in a main program or sub program architecture distributed among multiple computers on a network.
2. **Main program or Subprogram architectures:** The main program structure decomposes into number of subprograms or function into a control hierarchy. Main program contains number of subprograms that can invoke other components.

4. Object Oriented Architecture

The components of a system encapsulate data and the operations that must be applied to manipulate the data. The coordination and communication between the components are established via the message passing.

Characteristics of Object Oriented architecture

- Object protect the system's integrity.
- An object is unaware of the depiction of other items.

5. Layered Architecture

- A number of different layers are defined with each layer performing a well-defined set of operations. Each layer will do some operations that becomes closer to machine instruction set progressively.
- At the outer layer, components will receive the user interface operations and at the inner layers, components will perform the operating system interfacing(communication and coordination with OS)
- Intermediate layers to utility services and application software functions.

Example: E-Commerce System Architecture

- **Architecture:** Microservices-Based
  - **User Service:** Handles user authentication
  - **Product Service:** Manages product catalog
  - **Order Service:** Handles orders & payments
  - **Notification Service:** Sends email/SMS notifications
  - **Database:** Stores customer, product, and order data.

3.4.1 Pipe and Filter Architecture - System Design

In system design, the Pipe and Filter architecture structures processing tasks into a sequence of stages known as "pipes," where each stage filters and transforms data incrementally. This modular framework enables filters to operate independently, improving scalability and reusability.

Each filter is tasked with specific operations, such as validating or formatting data, and passes its output to the next stage via interconnected pipes.

What is Pipe and Filter Architecture?

The Pipe and Filter architecture is a design pattern that divides a process into a series of distinct steps, called filters, linked by channels known as pipes. Each filter is dedicated to a particular processing function, whether it involves transforming, validating, or aggregating data. Data flows through these filters via pipes, which carry the output of one filter to the input of another.

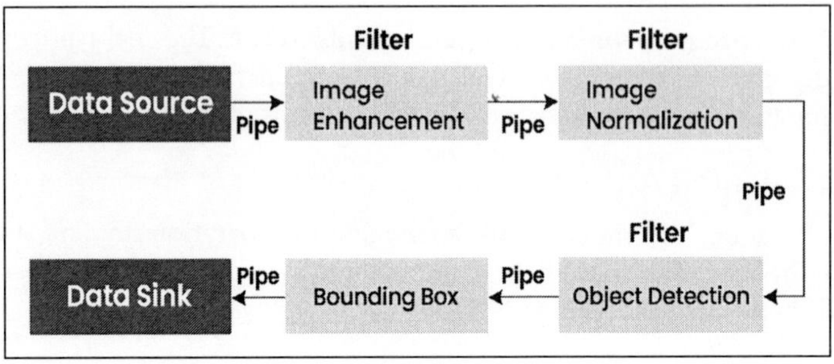

Figure 3.4

This architecture enhances modularity, as each filter operates independently and concentrates on a singular function. It also promotes reusability, allowing filters to be utilized across different systems or applications.

Pipe and Filter Architecture

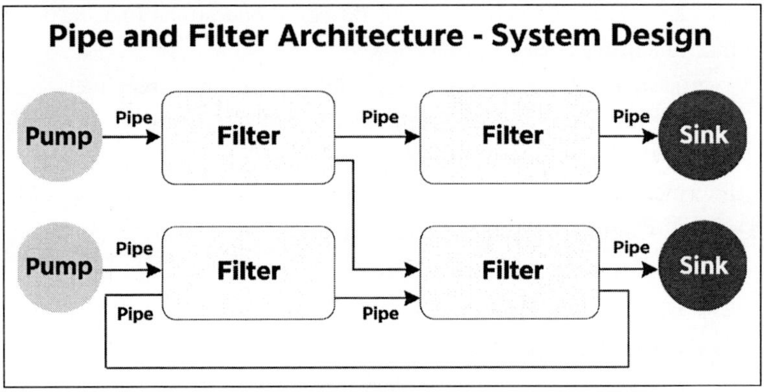

Figure 3.5

The architecture is highly modular, with each filter functioning independently, simplifying system comprehension, maintenance, and expansion. Filters can be added, removed, or rearranged without significant impact on the overall system, and parallel pipelines can boost throughput for larger data volumes.

1. **Pumps:** These components initiate the process by acting as data sources, injecting data into the system and starting the flow through the pipeline.
2. **Filters:** Each filter carries out a specific, standalone task, whether it be transforming, validating, or processing data before forwarding it. In the setup, there are two levels of filters; the first one processes data from the pump and hands it to the second filter, which continues the processing before passing it on.

3. **Pipes:** Pipes serve as the channels for data movement between filters, linking each component in sequence and ensuring a smooth transfer of data. In diagrams, pipes are depicted as arrows connecting the components.
4. **Sinks:** These are the endpoints where the processed data is ultimately collected or utilized. After passing through all filters, the data arrives at the sink, completing its pipeline journey.

Characteristics of Pipe and Filter Architecture

The Pipe and Filter architecture in system design possesses several key characteristics that make it an effective and popular design pattern for many applications. Here are its main characteristics:

- **Modularity:** Each filter is a standalone component that performs a specific task. This separation allows for easy understanding, development, and maintenance of individual filters without affecting the entire system.
- **Reusability:** Filters can be reused across different systems or within different parts of the same system. This reduces duplication of effort and promotes efficient use of resources.
- **Composability:** Filters can be composed in various sequences to create complex processing pipelines. This flexibility allows designers to build customized workflows by simply reordering or combining filters.
- **Scalability:** The architecture supports parallel processing by running multiple instances of filters. This enhances the system's ability to handle larger data volumes and improves performance.
- **Maintainability:** Isolating functions into separate filters simplifies debugging and maintenance. Changes to one filter do not impact others, making updates and bug fixes easier to manage.

Implementation Strategies

Implementing the Pipe and Filter architecture requires a strategic approach to ensure the system is efficient, maintainable, and scalable. Here are detailed strategies for implementing this architecture:

- **Define Clear Interfaces:**
  - **Uniform Input/Output:** Establish consistent input and output formats for each filter to ensure smooth data flow between filters.
  - **Standardized Protocols:** Use standardized communication protocols (e.g., HTTP, gRPC) for inter-process communication.
- **Design Modular Filters:**
  - **Single Responsibility Principle:** Each filter should perform one specific task, making the system easier to manage and debug.
  - **Encapsulation:** Keep the internal logic of each filter hidden, exposing only necessary interfaces.
- **Stateless Filters:**
  - **Statelessness:** Design filters to be stateless whenever possible to simplify scaling and parallel processing.

- **State Management:** If state is necessary, manage it externally or ensure it›s isolated and does not affect other filters.

- **Testing and Validation:**
  - **Unit Testing**: Thoroughly test each filter independently to ensure it performs its intended function correctly.
  - **Integration Testing:** Validate the entire pipeline to ensure filters work together seamlessly and data flows correctly.
- **Security Considerations:**
  - **Data Encryption:** Ensure data is encrypted in transit and at rest to protect sensitive information.
  - **Access Controls:** Implement strict access controls to prevent unauthorized access to filters and data.

Real-world Examples

The Pipe and Filter architecture is employed in a variety of real-world systems across different domains. Here are some notable examples:

- **Unix/Linux Command Line:**
  - **Shell Pipelines:** Unix and Linux shells (e.g., Bash) allow users to chain commands together using pipes. For example, cat file.txt | grep "pattern" | sort | uniq processes a file through a series of commands to filter, sort, and remove duplicates.
- **Compilers:**
  - **GCC (GNU Compiler Collection):** GCC processes source code through several stages including preprocessing, parsing, optimization, and code generation. Each stage is a filter that transforms the code from one form to another.

In conclusion, the Pipe and Filter architecture offers a powerful way to design systems by breaking down tasks into reusable components (filters) connected through channels (pipes). It promotes modularity, allowing developers to independently develop, test, and maintain each filter. This approach enhances scalability, flexibility, and maintainability across various domains like data processing, stream processing, web development, and more.

3.4.2 Call and Return Systems (Hierarchical Architecture)

A Call and Return System is a hierarchical software architecture where a main module (caller) invokes submodules (called functions), processes the result, and continues execution. This design promotes modularity, reuse, and structured programming.The "call and return" system design is a fundamental architectural style in software engineering, representing a classic method of program control. Here's a breakdown of its characteristics.

Core Concept

- **Hierarchical Control:**
  - At its essence, a call and return system involves a hierarchical control structure. One component (the "caller") invokes another component (the "callee") to perform a specific task.

- After the callee completes its task, it "returns" control to the caller, often providing a result or data.

The "call and return" system design is a fundamental architectural style in software engineering, representing a classic method of program control. Here's a breakdown of its characteristics:

Key Characteristics

- **Procedural Flow:**
  - This design emphasizes a sequential, procedural flow of control. The program's execution follows a well-defined path of calls and returns.
- **Modularity:**
  - It promotes modularity by breaking down complex tasks into smaller, reusable components (functions, procedures, subroutines).
- **Structured Programming:**
  - Call and return is closely associated with structured programming principles, which emphasize clear, organized, and predictable code.
- **Stack-Based Execution:**
  - Typically, call and return mechanisms rely on a stack data structure to manage the flow of control. When a call occurs, the caller's state is pushed onto the stack, and when the callee returns, the state is popped off the stack.

Examples

1. Traditional procedural programming languages (like C) heavily utilize call and return.
2. Function calls in most programming languages adhere to this model.
3. Remote Procedure Calls (RPCs) extend this concept to distributed systems.

Call and Return systems provide a **structured, modular** approach to software design. They are best suited for **layered architectures, procedural and object-oriented programming**, but can be limiting in **highly distributed systems**.

```
class Car {
    void start() { System.out.println("Car Started!"); }
}

public class Main {
    public static void main(String[] args) {
        Car myCar = new Car();
        myCar.start(); // Call and return
    }
}
```

It is used to create a program that is easy to scale and modify. Many sub-styles exist within this category. Two of them are explained below.

- **Remote procedure call architecture:** This components is used to present in a main program or sub program architecture distributed among multiple computers on a network.

- **Main program or Subprogram architectures:** The main program structure decomposes into number of subprograms or function into a control hierarchy. Main program contains number of subprograms that can invoke other components.

Advantages

- Simple and predictable control flow.
- Highly modular, improving maintainability.
- Supports reuse of functions and objects.

Disadvantages

- Tightly coupled, making changes harder in large systems.
- Stack Overhead, especially with deep recursive calls.
- Limited Scalability compared to event-driven or microservices-based architectures

3.4.3 Object-oriented systems

Object Oriented System is a type of development model where Objects are used to specify different aspects of an application. Everything including Data, information, processes, functions, and so on is considered an object in Object-Oriented System.

Object Oriented System, the software developer focuses on the task, not on the tools and it organizes the application on the basis of Object-Oriented Concepts. The behavior of the System depends on the collaboration between different Objects. As we go further to Design any system, there are four major Phases of Software Development using Object-Oriented Development

Phases of Object-Oriented Software Development

Object-Oriented Development is a structured approach to design and build software systems using the principle of Object-Oriented Programming(OOP). The Process of designing a system consists of several Phases, which help to ensure that the system is well-designed, and meets all the requirements of the user. Phases of the Object-Oriented Approach promote modularity, and reusability which helps developers to manage the system easily throughout the cycle.

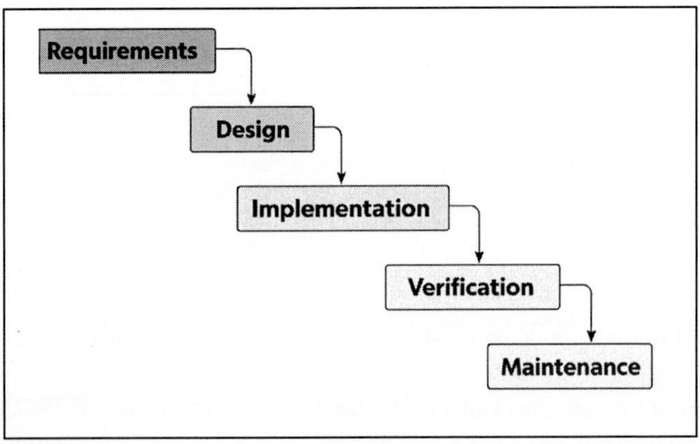

Figure 3.6

Object Oriented Design includes both

- System Design
- Object Design

System Design

System Design is critical part in Object Oriented Design where we design a Software System based on the information gathered during Analysis of the requirement of the Software. System Design focuses on the roadmap that provides how various components and modules of the software will work together. Designing a system is done according to both Analysis and the purposed Architecture of system

Object Design

Object Design is critical part of Object-Oriented Design where the main focus is on the detailed design of individual Classes and Objects, Specifying how they are Implemented on the System design of Software Development. Object Design is the foundation of writing Actual Code for the Software Development and it must be ensured that system is efficient, easily maintainable and extensible.

```
+----------+
|    Book      |
+----------+
|  - Title      |
|  - Author   |
| - Available|
+----------+
```

Figure 3.7

Object-Oriented Implementation

Object Oriented Implementation is a Phase in Software Development where the design model and the Structure that is developed in Object Oriented Analysis and Object oriented Design is translated into actual Code using Appropriate Programming Language. In this phase we convert the design and structure of software into actual code using an Object Oriented Programming Languages (OOPS) such as JAVA, C++ etc.

Advantages

- **Reusability:** Code can be reused via inheritance
- **Scalability:** Easy to extend by adding new objects/classes
- **Modularity:** Separation of concerns makes the system easy to manage
- **Security:** Data hiding (encapsulation) improves security

Disadvantages

- **Increased Complexity:** Designing OOS requires deep planning
- **Memory Overhead:** Objects and classes take up more memory
- **Slower Execution:** Compared to procedural programming

3.4.4 Layered Systems

Software engineering is a fully layered technology, to develop software we need to go from one layer to another. All the layers are connected and each layer demands the fulfillment of the previous layer.

Layered systems architecture is a common and widely used design pattern in software engineering. It involves organizing a system into distinct, horizontal layers, each with a specific role and responsibility. Here's a breakdown of its key characteristics:

Core Concepts

- **Separation of Concerns:** Each layer handles a specific set of functionalities, minimizing dependencies between different parts of the system.
- **Hierarchical Structure:** Layers are arranged in a hierarchical order, with each layer typically interacting only with the layers immediately above and below it.
- **Abstraction:** Each layer provides an abstraction of the services it offers, hiding the underlying implementation details from other layers.

Typical Layers

While the specific layers can vary depending on the system, common examples include:

- **Presentation Layer:** Handles user interface and user interaction.
- **Application Layer (Business Logic Layer):** Implements the core business logic and workflows of the application.
- **Domain Layer:** Contains the business entities, and business rules.
- **Data Access Layer (Persistence Layer):** Manages data storage and retrieval, interacting with databases or other data sources.
- **Infrastructure Layer:** Provides supporting technical services, such as networking, file systems, and logging.

Layered architecture is a valuable design pattern that promotes modularity, maintainability, and scalability. It's widely used in various software applications, from web applications to enterprise systems.

Example: Layered Architecture in a Web Application

- **Presentation Layer:** UserController handles user requests.
- **Business Logic Layer:** UserService processes requests.
- **Data Layer:** UserRepository fetches data from the database.

Advantages & Disadvantages

Advantages

- **Modular and Maintainable:** Changes in one layer do not affect others.
- **Scalable:** Can add more layers as needed.
- **Improved Security:** Layers can enforce access control and validation.

Disadvantages

- **Performance Overhead:** Extra layers can slow down execution.
- **Rigid Structure:** May not be ideal for real-time or highly dynamic systems.
- **Tightly Coupled Layers:** Some layers depend heavily on others, making changes difficult.

Key Takeaway: Layered systems enhance modularity, maintainability, and scalability by structuring software into distinct, independent layers. They are widely used in enterprise applications, networking, and distributed systems, but may introduce performance trade-offs.

3.4.5 Data Centered Systems

A Data-Centered System is a software architecture where data is the central component, and all other components (modules or services) interact with this central data repository. It is commonly used in database management systems (DBMS), enterprise applications, and cloud-based platforms.

Key Characteristics of Data-Centered Systems

- **Centralized Data Management:** A single, shared data source is used by multiple components.
- **Loose Coupling:** Components interact via the centralized data store rather than direct connections.
- **Scalability & Reliability:** Data can be scaled and maintained efficiently.
- **High Data Integrity:** Changes to data are consistent and synchronized across all modules.

Examples

- **Database Management Systems (DBMS):** MySQL, PostgreSQL
- **Enterprise Resource Planning (ERP):** SAP, Oracle ERP
- **Cloud Storage Solutions:** Google Drive, AWS S3

Data-Centered vs. Other Architectures

Aspect	Data-Centered Systems	Layered Systems	Client-Server
Central Component	Data Repository	Layers (Presentation, Logic, Data)	Server
Coupling	Loose Coupling	Medium	Medium
Data Flow	Components interact with a central database	Data flows through layers	Clients request from server
Scalability	High	Medium	High
Best For	DBMS, AI, ERP, Cloud Storage	Web Apps, OS	Web Apps, APIs

Why This Approach?

1. Data is Valuable

In today's world, data is a critical asset. Data-centered systems recognize this and treat data accordingly.

2. Consistency

Centralizing data helps to ensure that everyone is working with the same information.

3. Efficiency

By focusing on data, systems can be optimized for data storage, retrieval, and analysis.

Examples

1. Database Systems

Relational databases are a classic example of data-centered systems.

2. Data Warehouses

These systems consolidate data from various sources for analysis.

3. Data Lakes

These store large volumes of raw data in various formats.

Data-centered systems are about building systems where data is not just an afterthought, but the central organizing principle. This approach is becoming increasingly important as organizations grapple with ever-growing volumes of data.

3.5 Structured Analysis and Structured Design:

Structured Analysis and Structured Design (SA/SD) is a diagrammatic notation that is designed to help people understand the system. The basic goal of SA/SD is to improve quality and reduce the risk of system failure. It establishes concrete management specifications and documentation. It focuses on the solidity, pliability, and maintainability of the system.

In SA/SD, the software development process is divided into two phases: Structured Analysis and Structured Design. During the Structured Analysis phase, the problem to be solved is analyzed and the requirements are gathered. The Structured Design phase involves designing the system to meet the requirements that were gathered in the Structured Analysis phase.

- **Functional Decomposition:** SA/SD uses functional decomposition to break down a complex system into smaller, more manageable subsystems. This technique involves identifying the main functions of the system and breaking them down into smaller functions that can be implemented independently.
- **Data Flow Diagrams (DFDs):** SA/SD uses DFDs to model the flow of data through the system. DFDs are graphical representations of the system that show how data moves between the system's various components.
- **Data Dictionary:** A data dictionary is a central repository that contains descriptions of all the data elements used in the system. It provides a clear and consistent definition of data elements, making it easier to understand how the system works.
- **Structured Design:** SA/SD uses structured design techniques to develop the system's architecture and components. It involves identifying the major components of the system, designing the interfaces between them, and specifying the data structures and algorithms that will be used to implement the system.
- **Modular Programming:** SA/SD uses modular programming techniques to break down the system's code into smaller, more manageable modules. This makes it easier to develop, test, and maintain the system.

SA/SD involves 2 phases:

- **Analysis Phase:** It uses Data Flow Diagram, Data Dictionary, State Transition diagram and ER diagram.
- **Design Phase:** It uses Structure Chart and Pseudo Code.

1. Analysis Phase

Analysis Phase involves data flow diagram, data dictionary, state transition diagram, and entity-relationship diagram.

- **Data Flow Diagram:** In the data flow diagram, the model describes how the data flows through the system. We can incorporate the Boolean operators and & or link data flow when more than one data flow may be input or output from a process.
- **Data Dictionary**: The content that is not described in the DFD is described in the data dictionary. It defines the data store and relevant meaning. A physical data dictionary for data elements that flow between processes, between entities, and between processes and entities may be included. This would also include descriptions of data elements that flow external to the data stores.
- **State Transition Diagram**: State transition diagram is similar to the dynamic model. It specifies how much time the function will take to execute and data access triggered by events. It also describes all of the states that an object can have, the events under which an object changes state, the conditions that must be fulfilled before the transition will occur and the activities were undertaken during the life of an object.
- **ER Diagram:** ER diagram specifies the relationship between data store. It is basically used in database design. It basically describes the relationship between different entities.

2. Design Phase

Design Phase involves structure chart and pseudocode.

- **Structure Chart**: It is created by the data flow diagram. Structure Chart specifies how DFS's processes are grouped into tasks and allocated to the CPU. The structured chart does not show the working and internal structure of the processes or modules and does not show the relationship between data or data flows. Similar to other SASD tools, it is time and cost-independent and there is no error-checking technique associated with this tool.
- **Pseudo Code**: It is the actual implementation of the system. It is an informal way of programming that doesn't require any specific programming language or technology.

3.5.1 Principles

Structured design principles are fundamental guidelines that aim to create well-organized, maintainable, and efficient software systems. These principles emphasize a systematic approach to breaking down complex problems into manageable modules. Here's a breakdown of key structured design principles.

Core Principles

- **Modularization:** This is the cornerstone of structured design. It involves dividing a system into distinct, self-contained modules, each with a specific function. This promotes:
    - Code reusability.
    - Simplified maintenance.
    - Easier debugging.

Top-Down Design

- This approach begins with a high-level overview of the system and progressively refines it into more detailed components. It allows for:
  - Clear understanding of the system's overall structure.
  - Systematic decomposition of complex tasks.

Structured Programming

- This principle advocates for the use of control structures that promote clarity and predictability, such as:
  - **Sequence:** Executing instructions in a linear order.
  - **Selection:** Using "if-then-else" statements for decision-making.
  - **Iteration:** Employing loops for repetitive tasks.

Cohesion

This refers to the degree to which the elements within a module are related. High cohesion is desirable, as it indicates that a module performs a single, well-defined task.

Coupling

This measures the degree of interdependence between modules. Low coupling is desirable, as it minimizes the impact of changes in one module on other modules.

Key Concepts in Practice

1. Data Flow Diagrams (DFDs)

These visual representations illustrate how data moves through a system, aiding in understanding data transformations.

2. Structure Charts

These diagrams depict the hierarchical organization of modules and their relationships, providing a clear view of the system's architecture.

Importance

These principles contribute to creating software that is:

- Easier to understand.
- Simpler to modify.
- More reliable.

Although modern software development incorporates various paradigms, the fundamental principles of structured design remain relevant for creating well-structured and maintainable software.Key Takeaway: Structured Design is a function-driven approach that emphasizes modularity, low coupling, high cohesion, and information hiding. It is widely used in business applications, banking systems, and database-driven applications.

3.6 Strategies for Converting DFD Into Structure Chart

Converting Data Flow Diagrams (DFDs) into Structure Charts is a crucial step in structured design. Here's a breakdown of strategies and techniques for this conversion:

1. Transform Analysis (Transactional Analysis)

- **Identify Transaction Centres:**
  - Look for DFD processes that receive input and dispatch it to various processing paths based on the input type. These are transaction centers.
  - Each transaction center becomes a main control module in the Structure Chart.
- **Create a Transaction Center Module:**
  - The transaction center module controls the dispatching of transactions.
- **Create Subordinate Modules:** For each transaction path in the DFD, create a corresponding subordinate module in the Structure Chart.
- **Establish Data Flow:** Represent data flow between modules using connectors and data couples in the Structure Chart.

Transform Analysis (Transform-Centered Analysis)

- **Identify the Central Transform:** Locate the DFD processes that perform the core transformations on the input data. This is the central transform.
- **Create a Main Control Module:** The central transform becomes the main control module in the Structure Chart.
- **Identify Input and Output Streams:** Determine the input and output streams of data leading into and out of the central transform.

General Conversion Strategies

- **Map Processes to Modules:** Each process in the DFD generally becomes a module in the Structure Chart.
- **Map Data Flows to Data Couples:** Data flows between processes in the DFD become data couples (parameters) passed between modules in the Structure Chart.
- **Map Data Stores to Data Access Modules:** Data stores in the DFD may become data access modules in the Structure Chart, responsible for reading and writing data.

Key Considerations

- **Clarity and Readability:** The Structure Chart should be clear and easy to understand.
- **Maintainability:** The design should facilitate easy maintenance and modification.
- **Efficiency:** The design should consider performance and efficiency.

By following these strategies and principles, you can effectively convert DFDs into Structure Charts, creating a well-structured and maintainable software design.

Best Practices for Converting DFD to SC

- Use a top-down approach: Start from the main module and decompose.
- Keep modules small and focused: Follow high cohesion, low coupling principles.
- Ensure well-defined module interfaces: Clearly define input/output data.
- Use control modules wisely: Implement conditions and decisions at the appropriate level.

- Map data stores correctly: Ensure database interactions are handled via specific data access modules.

3.7 How to Measure the Goodness of the Design

Measuring the "goodness" of a software design is a multifaceted endeavor, encompassing both qualitative and quantitative assessments. It's about evaluating how well a design fulfills its intended purpose while adhering to sound engineering principles. Here's a breakdown of key measurement strategies.

1. Qualitative Measures

Maintainability

This assesses how easily the design can be modified or repaired. Factors include:

1. **Readability:** How clear and understandable is the code?
2. **Modularity:** How well is the system broken down into independent modules?
3. **Complexity:** How intricate is the design? Simpler designs are generally more maintainable.

Usability

This focuses on how effectively users can interact with the system. It involves:

1. **User testing:** Observing users as they perform tasks.
2. **Feedback collection:** Gathering user opinions through surveys and interviews.

Flexibility

This evaluates how easily the design can adapt to changing requirements.

Clarity and Understandability

- How easy is it for other developers to understand the design. This can be measured through code reviews, and documentation reviews.

Adherence to Principles

- How well does the design adhere to established design principles (e.g., SOLID principles, DRY principle)?

Code Reviews

- Expert evaluation of the code and design to find flaws, and areas of improvement.

2. Quantitative Measures

- **Coupling and Cohesion:** Measuring the degree of interdependence between modules (coupling) and the degree of relatedness within modules (cohesion).
  - Low coupling and high cohesion are generally desirable.
- **Complexity Metrics:** Using metrics like cyclomatic complexity to assess the complexity of code.
- **Performance Metrics:** Measuring factors like response time, throughput, and resource utilization.

- **Error Rate:** Tracking the number of defects or errors that occur during testing and in production.
- **Test Coverage:** Measuring the percentage of code that is covered by tests.
- **Scalability Metrics:**
  - Measuring how well the system handles increased load.

3. User-Centric Measures

- **Net Promoter Score (NPS):** Measures customer loyalty and satisfaction.
- **Customer Satisfaction (CSAT):** Gauges overall customer satisfaction with the system.
- **Task Success Rate:** Measures the percentage of users who can successfully complete specific tasks.
- **Time on Task:** Measures how long it takes users to complete specific tasks.

By employing these measurement strategies, software engineers can gain valuable insights into the quality of their designs and make informed decisions to improve them.

Software Metrics for Measuring Design Quality

Metric	Description	Good Design Criteria
Cyclomatic Complexity	Measures code complexity.	Lower is better.
**Depth of Ingeritance Tree (DIT)		

3.7.1 Coupling and Cohesion

The purpose of the Design phase in the Software Development Life Cycle is to produce a solution to a problem given in the SRS(Software Requirement Specification) document. The output of the design phase is a Software Design Document (SDD).

Coupling and Cohesion are two key concepts in software engineering that are used to measure the quality of a software system's design.

What is Coupling and Cohesion? Coupling refers to the degree of interdependence between software modules. High coupling means that modules are closely connected and changes in one module may affect other modules. Low coupling means that modules are independent, and changes in one module have little impact on other modules.

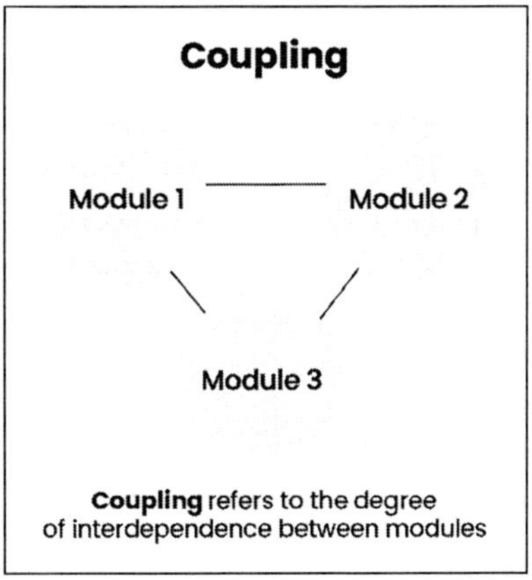

Figure 3.8

3.7.2 Cohesion

refers to the degree to which elements within a module work together to fulfil a single, well-defined purpose. High cohesion means that elements are closely related and focused on a single purpose, while low cohesion means that elements are loosely related and serve multiple purposes.

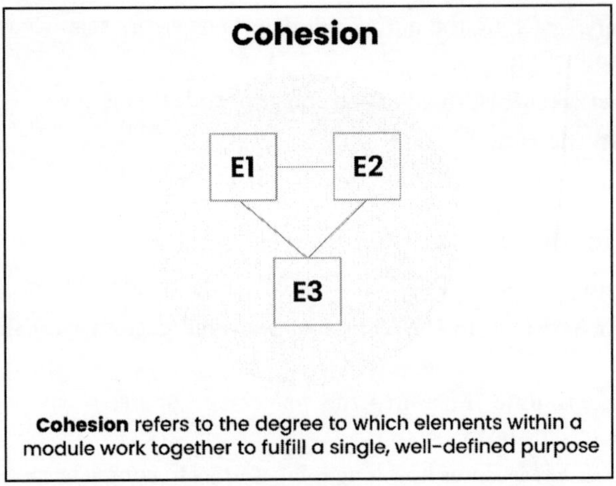

Figure 3.9

Both coupling and cohesion are important factors in determining the maintainability, scalability, and reliability of a software system. High coupling and low cohesion can make a system difficult to change and test, while low coupling and high cohesion make a system easier to maintain and improve.

Basically, design is a two-part iterative process. The first part is Conceptual Design which tells the customer what the system will do. Second is Technical Design which allows the system builders to understand the actual hardware and software needed to solve a customer's problem.

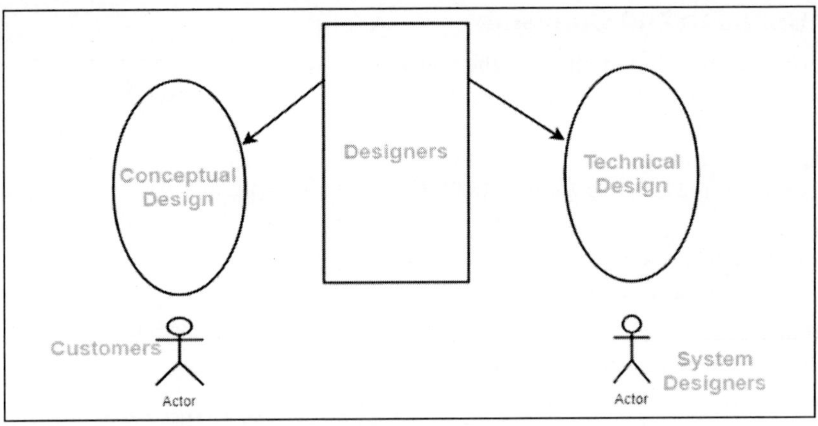

Figure 3.10

Conceptual Design of the System

Written in simple language i.e. customer understandable language.

- Detailed explanation about system characteristics.
- Describes the functionality of the system.
- It is independent of implementation.
- Linked with requirement document.

Technical Design of the System

- Hardware component and design.
- Functionality and hierarchy of software components.
- Software architecture
- Network architecture
- Data structure and flow of data.
- I/O component of the system.
- Shows interface.

Modularization is the process of dividing a software system into multiple independent modules where each module works independently. There are many advantages of Modularization in software engineering.

3.7.3 Types of Coupling

Following are the types of Coupling:

- **Data Coupling:** If the dependency between the modules is based on the fact that they communicate by passing only data, then the modules are said to be data coupled. In data coupling, the components are independent of each other and communicate through data. Module communications don't contain tramp data. Example-customer billing system.
- **Stamp Coupling** In stamp coupling, the complete data structure is passed from one module to another module. Therefore, it involves tramp data. It may be necessary due to efficiency factors- this choice was made by the insightful designer, not a lazy programmer.

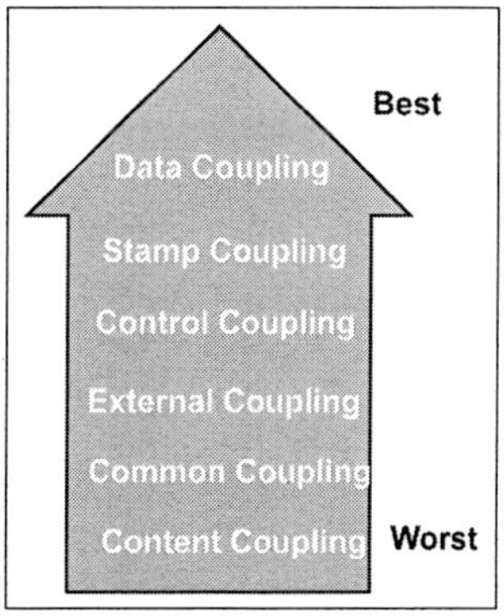

Figure 3.11

- **Control Coupling:** If the modules communicate by passing control information, then they are said to be control coupled. It can be bad if parameters indicate completely different behavior and good if parameters allow factoring and reuse of functionality.

  Example: sort function that takes comparison function as an argument.
- **External Coupling:** In external coupling, the modules depend on other modules, external to the software being developed or to a particular type of hardware. Ex-protocol, external file, device format, etc.
- **Common Coupling:** The modules have shared data such as global data structures. The changes in global data mean tracing back to all modules which access that data to evaluate the effect of the change. So it has got disadvantages like difficulty in reusing modules, reduced ability to control data accesses, and reduced maintainability.
- **Content Coupling:** In a content coupling, one module can modify the data of another module, or control flow is passed from one module to the other module. This is the worst form of coupling and should be avoided.

- **Temporal Coupling:** Temporal coupling occurs when two modules depend on the timing or order of events, such as one module needing to execute before another. This type of coupling can result in design issues and difficulties in testing and maintenance.
- **Sequential Coupling:** Sequential coupling occurs when the output of one module is used as the input of another module, creating a chain or sequence of dependencies. This type of coupling can be difficult to maintain and modify.
- **Communicational Coupling:** Communicational coupling occurs when two or more modules share a common communication mechanism, such as a shared message queue or database. This type of coupling can lead to performance issues and difficulty in debugging.
- **Functional Coupling:** Functional coupling occurs when two modules depend on each other's functionality, such as one module calling a function from another module. This type of coupling can result in tightly-coupled code that is difficult to modify and maintain.
- **Data-Structured Coupling:** Data-structured coupling occurs when two or more modules share a common data structure, such as a database table or data file. This type of coupling can lead to difficulty in maintaining the integrity of the data structure and can result in performance issues.
- **Interaction Coupling**: Interaction coupling occurs due to the methods of a class invoking methods of other classes. Like with functions, the worst form of coupling here is if methods directly access internal parts of other methods. Coupling is lowest if methods communicate directly through parameters.
- **Component Coupling:** Component coupling refers to the interaction between two classes where a class has variables of the other class. Three clear situations exist as to how this can happen. A class C can be component coupled with another class C1, if C has an instance variable of type C1, or C has a method whose parameter is of type C1,or if C has a method which has a local variable of type C1. It should be clear that whenever there is component coupling, there is likely to be interaction coupling.

Types of Cohesion

- **Functional Cohesion:** Every essential element for a single computation is contained in the component. A functional cohesion performs the task and functions. It is an ideal situation.
- **Sequential Cohesion:** An element outputs some data that becomes the input for other element, i.e., data flow between the parts. It occurs naturally in functional programming languages.
- **Communicational Cohesion:** Two elements operate on the same input data or contribute towards the same output data. Example- update record in the database and send it to the printer.

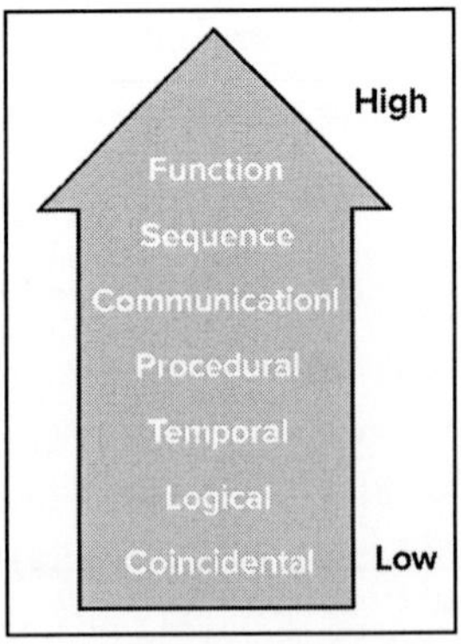

Figure 3.12

- **Procedural Cohesion:** Elements of procedural cohesion ensure the order of execution. Actions are still weakly connected and unlikely to be reusable. Ex- calculate student GPA, print student record, calculate cumulative GPA, print cumulative GPA.
- **Temporal Cohesion:** The elements are related by their timing involved. A module connected with temporal cohesion all the tasks must be executed in the same time span. This cohesion contains the code for initializing all the parts of the system. Lots of different activities occur, all at unit time.
- **Logical Cohesion:** The elements are logically related and not functionally. Ex- A component reads inputs from tape, disk, and network. All the code for these functions is in the same component. Operations are related, but the functions are significantly different.
- **Coincidental Cohesion:** The elements are not related(unrelated). The elements have no conceptual relationship other than location in source code. It is accidental and the worst form of cohesion. Ex- print next line and reverse the characters of a string in a single component.
- **Procedural Cohesion:** This type of cohesion occurs when elements or tasks are grouped together in a module based on their sequence of execution, such as a module that performs a set of related procedures in a specific order. Procedural cohesion can be found in structured programming languages.

In conclusion, it's good for software to have low coupling and high cohesion. Low coupling means the different parts of the software don't rely too much on each other, which makes it safer to make changes without causing unexpected problems. High cohesion means each part of the software has a clear purpose and sticks to it, making the code easier to work with and reuse. Following these principles helps make software stronger, more adaptable, and easier to grow.

This page is intentionally left blank!

TESTING

4

UNIT

4.1 Software Testing Fundamentals

Software testing fundamentals involve the essential principles, methodologies, and processes used to ensure software quality, reliability, and performance. It is a systematic approach to identifying defects, verifying functionality, and ensuring the software meets user and business requirements. Testing is broadly classified into manual and automated testing, where manual testing relies on human intervention, while automated testing uses tools like Selenium, JUnit, and TestNG for efficiency. The software testing life cycle (STLC) consists of key phases, including requirement analysis, test planning, test case development, environment setup, test execution, and test closure.

Testing is conducted at multiple levels, such as unit testing for individual components, integration testing for module interactions, system testing for overall functionality, and acceptance testing to validate business needs. Different testing methodologies, including white-box, black-box, and gray-box testing, help evaluate software from both structural and functional perspectives. Additionally, various testing techniques such as functional, non-functional, regression, load, and security testing ensure performance, usability, and security compliance. Software testing is a crucial process in the software development lifecycle (SDLC) that ensures the quality, reliability, and performance of a software product. Here are the key fundamentals:

4.1.1 What is Software Testing?

Software testing is the process of evaluating a software application to ensure it meets specified requirements and functions correctly without defects. It involves executing the software under controlled conditions to identify bugs, errors, or any deviations from expected behaviour. The primary goal of software testing is to ensure the quality, reliability, security, and performance of the software before it is deployed for end users.

Testing can be conducted **manually**, where testers execute test cases without automation tools, or **automatically**, using tools like Selenium, JUnit, and TestNG to speed up testing processes. It is performed at different levels, including **unit testing** (testing individual components), **integration testing** (checking interactions between modules), **system testing** (validating the complete system), and **acceptance testing** (ensuring the software meets business requirements). Different testing methodologies, such as **black-box testing** (focusing on functionality), **white-box testing** (analyzing internal code), and **gray-box testing** (a mix of both), help in evaluating various aspects of the software.

Software testing is essential for preventing software failures, reducing maintenance costs, and ensuring user satisfaction by delivering a reliable and high-quality product.

4.1.2 Why is Testing Important?

Software testing is essential to ensure the quality, reliability, and performance of a software application. It helps detect and fix defects before deployment, reducing the risk of software failures that could lead to financial loss, security breaches, or poor user experience. Testing ensures that the software meets business and user requirements, functions correctly under various conditions, and provides a smooth and efficient experience.

Objectives of Software Testing

The primary objective of software testing is to ensure that a software application functions as intended, meets user and business requirements, and is free from defects.

Below are the key objectives of software testing:

- Detect and Fix Bugs
- Ensure Software Quality
- Validate Business Requirements
- Improve Security
- Enhance Performance

Detect and Fix Bugs

One of the primary objectives of software testing is to **detect and fix bugs** to ensure the software functions correctly and meets user requirements. Bugs are defects, errors, or flaws in a software application that cause it to behave unexpectedly or incorrectly. These defects can arise due to coding mistakes, design flaws, incorrect requirements, or integration issues.

Detecting and fixing bugs early in the development process reduces costs, improves software quality, and enhances user experience.

Ensure Software Quality

Ensuring software quality is a critical objective of software testing, as it guarantees that the application functions correctly, meets requirements, and delivers a seamless user experience. **Software quality** refers to the degree to which a software product meets customer expectations, is free of defects, and performs efficiently in various conditions.

By following a structured **Software Testing Life Cycle (STLC)** and using a mix of manual and automated testing methods, organizations can enhance software quality, reduce maintenance costs, and increase user satisfaction. High-quality software leads to better customer trust, competitive advantage, and long-term business success.

Improve Security

Security is a crucial aspect of software testing, as it ensures that an application is protected from vulnerabilities, cyber threats, and unauthorized access. Security testing helps identify weaknesses in the software that could be exploited by attackers, safeguarding sensitive data and maintaining user trust.

Enhance Performance

A multimodal strategy is needed to improve speed, beginning with careful code optimization to cut down on redundancies and streamline procedures. Indexing, query optimization, and strategic caching are key components of database efficiency. Underlying bottlenecks are addressed by system-level enhancements like network optimization and hardware upgrades. For iterative improvements, ongoing testing and monitoring including load and stress assessments provide vital information.

In the end, a comprehensive approach that takes into account hardware, software, and operational factors is necessary for long-lasting and notable performance improvements.

4.2 Testing Approaches

There are many different software testing methodologies, and each one has a specific function in guaranteeing the quality of software. Fundamentally, integration testing looks at the interactions between code components, whereas unit testing verifies each component separately.

The completely integrated system is then assessed by system testing in relation to predetermined criteria. Acceptance testing, which is frequently carried out by end users, verifies that the program satisfies user needs.

4.2.1. Black Box Testing

Definition

- Testing software **without knowing** the internal code structure.
- Focuses on **input and expected output**.

Techniques

- **Equivalence Partitioning:** Divides input into **valid & invalid** groups to reduce test cases.
- **Boundary Value Analysis (BVA):** Tests **extreme boundary values** (min & max).
- **State Transition Testing:** Checks **different states of the system** (e.g., login → checkout → payment).
- **Error Guessing:** Based on tester experience, guesses **possible failure points**.

Example

- **Scenario:** Testing an ATM **withdrawal feature**.
- **Test Case:** Insert a valid ATM card → Enter correct PIN → Withdraw money.
- **Expected Outcome:** Money is dispensed correctly.

Who Performs It?

- QA Testers & End Users

Purpose

- Validates functional behavior.
- Ensures software meets business requirements.
- Performed from a user's perspective.

4.2. 2 White Box Testing

Definition

- Testing software with **full knowledge of code structure**.
- Focuses on **internal logic, code paths, and conditions**.

Techniques

- **Basis Path Testing:** Ensures every independent path in the program is executed.
- **Control Flow Testing:** Checks loops, conditions, and branches.
- **Data Flow Testing:** Tracks variable usage & assignments.
- **Mutation Testing:** Modifies code slightly to check if tests detect changes.

Example

- **Scenario:** Testing an **e-commerce checkout algorithm**.
- **Test Case:** Check if the system correctly **calculates total price** based on cart items.
- **Expected Outcome:** The total price calculation is correct.

Who Performs It?

- Developers & Testers with coding knowledge

Purpose

- Ensures correct implementation of logic & algorithms.
- Detects code-level errors & security vulnerabilities.
- Improves code efficiency.

Grey Box Testing (Hybrid Approach)

Definition

- A combination of **Black Box & White Box testing**.
- Testers have **partial knowledge** of the system's internal structure.

Example

- Testing a **web application's login system** with knowledge of database queries.

Who Performs It?

- Testers with **limited coding knowledge**.

Purpose

- Helps in security, integration, and database testing.
- Detects defects in data flow between modules.

Comparison of Testing Approaches

Feature	Black Box Testing	White Box Testing	Grey Box Testing
Focus	Functionality & user experience	Internal logic & code structure	Partial code knowledge
Performed By	Testers & end users	Developers & testers	Testers with coding knowledge
Knowledge of Code?	✗ No	Yes	Partial
Techniques Used	Equivalence Partitioning, BVA, State Transition	Basis Path, Control Flow, Data Flow	Both Black & White Box techniques
Example	Testing ATM withdrawals	Checking a sorting algorithm	Testing login with database knowledge

Conclusion

- Black Box Testing ensures the system meets user requirements.
- White Box Testing verifies the internal logic & code correctness.
- Grey Box Testing bridges the gap between the two for better defect detection.

Software testing techniques ensure software quality by identifying defects early and improving user experience. They boost confidence that the software meets requirements. However, testing can be time-consuming, resource-heavy, and may have limited coverage. Automated testing has its limitations and requires maintenance. Despite these challenges, the benefitslike improved quality, reduced costs, and easier maintenancemake testing essential for successful software development.

Types Of Software Testing Techniques

There are two main categories of software testing techniques:

- **Static Testing Techniques:** These testing techniques that are used to find defects in an application under test without executing the code. Static Testing is done to avoid errors at an early stage of the development cycle thus reducing the cost of fixing them.
- **Dynamic Testing Techniques:** These testing techniques that are used to test the dynamic behavior of the application under test, that is by the execution of the code base. The main purpose of dynamic testing is to test the application with dynamic inputs- some of which may be allowed as per requirement (Positive testing) and some are not allowed (Negative Testing)

Software testing techniques are the ways employed to test the application under test against the functional or non-functional requirements gathered from business. Each testing technique helps to find a specific type of defect. For example, Techniques that may find structural defects might not be able to find the defects against the end-to-end business flow. Hence, multiple testing techniques are applied in a testing project to conclude it with acceptable quality.

Black Box Testing

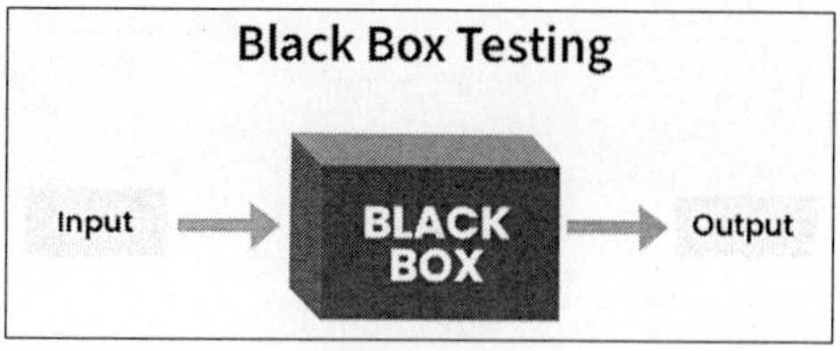

Figure 4.1

Black Box Testing is an important part of making sure software works as it should. Instead of exploring the code, testers check how the software behaves from the outside, just like users would. This helps catch any issues or bugs that might affect how the software works.

Black-box testing is a type of software testing in which the tester is not concerned with the software's internal knowledge or implementation details but rather focuses on validating the functionality based on the provided specifications or requirements.

Types Of Black Box Testing

The following are the various categories of black box testing:

- Functional Testing
- Regression Testing
- Nonfunctional Testing

Functional Testing

- Functional testing is defined as a type of testing that verifies that each function of the software application works in conformance with the requirement and specification.
- This testing is not concerned with the source code of the application.Each functionality of the software application is tested by providing appropriate test input, expecting the output, and comparing the actual output with the expected output.
- This testing focuses on checking the user interface, APIs, database, security, client or server application, and functionality of the Application Under Test. Functional testing can be manual or automated. It determines the system's software functional requirements.

Example

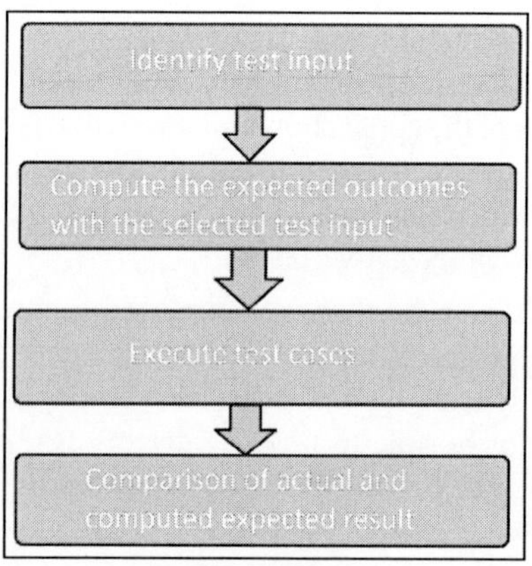

Figure 4.2

- Testing each and every indepently and throughly with respect to requirement. We perform functional testing for all components inside a module of an application.

Regression Testing

Regression testing is a crucial aspect of software engineering that ensures the stability and reliability of a software product. It involves retesting the previously tested functionalities to verify that recent code changes haven't adversely affected the existing features.By identifying and fixing any regression or unintended bugs, regression testing helps maintain the overall quality of the software. This process is essential for software development teams to deliver consistent and high-quality products to their users.

When to do Regression Testing?

- When new functionality is added to the system and the code has been modified to absorb and integrate that functionality with the existing code.
- When some defect has been identified in the software and the code is debugged to fix it. When the code is modified to optimize its working.

Process of Regression Testing

Firstly, whenever we make some changes to the source code for any reason like adding new functionality, optimization, etc. then our program when executed fails in the previously designed test suite for obvious reasons. After the failure, the source code is debugged to identify the bugs in the program.

After identification of the bugs in the source code, appropriate modifications are made. Then appropriate test cases are selected from the already existing test suite which covers all the modified and affected parts of the source code. We can add new test cases if required. In the end, regression testing is performed using the selected test cases.

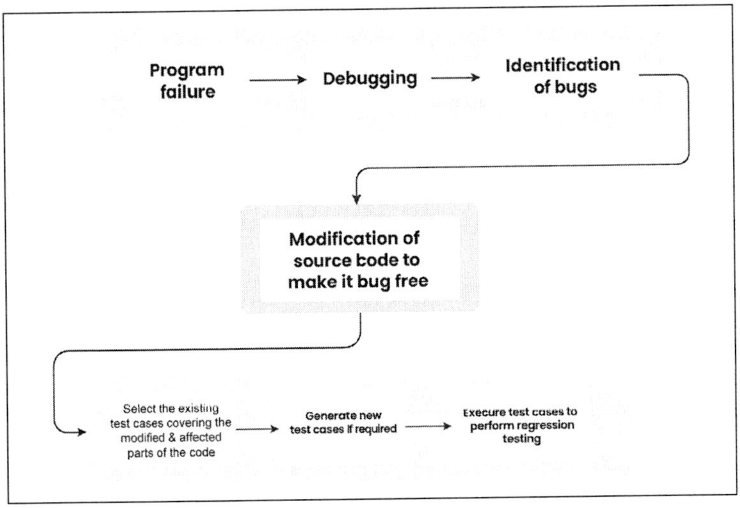

Figure 4.3

Regression testing is like a safety net for software changes, making sure they do not bring in new problems. It picks test cases from existing suites, sometimes focusing on modified parts.

Non-functional Testing

Behaviour Non-functional Testing is a type of Software Testing that is performed to verify the non-functional requirements of the application. It verifies whether the behaviour of the system is as per the requirement or not. It tests all the aspects that are not tested in functional testing.

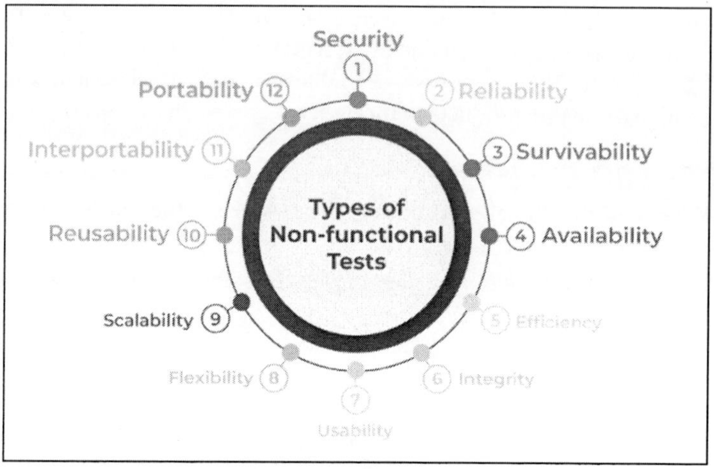

Figure 4.4

Non-functional testing is a software testing technique that checks the non-functional attributes of the system. Non-functional testing is defined as a type of software testing to check non-functional aspects of a software application. It is designed to test the readiness of a system as per nonfunctional parameters which are never addressed by functional testing. Non-functional testing is as important as functional testing.

Non-functional Testing Parameters

Non-functional testing check that the software meets the requirement, security, and performance standards. While it improves the user experience and security, it can be want the resources and costly during updates. Overall, it is a crucial for delivering a reliable and easy development the software product.

Equivalence Partitioning

Equivalence Partitioning Method is also known as Equivalence class partitioning (ECP). It is a software testing technique or black-box testing that divides input domain into classes of data, and with the help of these classes of data, test cases can be derived. An ideal test case identifies class of error that might require many arbitrary test cases to be executed before general error is observed.

In equivalence partitioning, equivalence classes are evaluated for given input conditions. Whenever any input is given, then type of input condition is checked, then for this input conditions, Equivalence class represents or describes set of valid or invalid states.

Guidelines for Equivalence Partitioning

- If the range condition is given as an input, then one valid and two invalid equivalence classes are defined.

- If a specific value is given as input, then one valid and two invalid equivalence classes are defined.
- If a member of set is given as an input, then one valid and one invalid equivalence class is defined.
- If Boolean no. is given as an input condition, then one valid and one invalid equivalence class is defined.

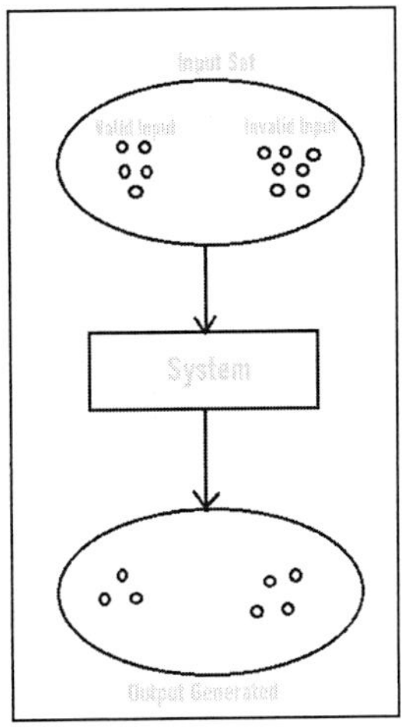

Figure 4.5

Key Idea

- Reduce the number of test cases while maintaining good coverage.
- Detect **invalid input handling** effectively.
- Saves time by avoiding redundant tests.

Example 1: Age Validation

A system accepts age between **18 and 60**.

Partition Type	Input Range	Representative Test Cases
Valid	18 - 60	18, 30, 60
Invalid (Too Low)	< 18	17
Invalid (Too High)	> 60	61

Why?

- Any number **below 18** should be rejected.
- Any number **above 60** should be rejected.
- Testing with just **one value** from each partition is sufficient.

Example 2: Login Password Length

A system requires a **password of 8-12 characters**.

Partition Type	Input Range	Representative Test Cases
Valid	8 - 12 characters	"Password1" (10 chars)
Invalid (Too Low)	< 8 chars	"Pass" (4 chars)
Invalid (Too High)	> 12 chars	"VeryLongPassword" (16 chars)

Why?

- Testing every possible length is inefficient.
- Instead, one valid, one too short, and one too long test case is enough.

When to Use Equivalence Partitioning?

- When testing forms, inputs, validation rules.
- When inputs have defined valid and invalid ranges.
- When optimizing test cases while ensuring good coverage.

Advantages of Equivalence Partitioning

- Fewer test cases with maximum coverage.
- Saves time by avoiding redundant tests.
- Works well for valid and invalid input testing.
- Helps quickly identify defects related to input validation.

Disadvantages of Equivalence Partitioning

- May miss edge cases (use Boundary Value Analysis to cover them).
- Does not test internal logic, only functional behavior.

Boundary Value Analysis

Boundary Value Analysis (BVA) is a black-box testing technique that focuses on testing the edges (boundaries) of input ranges. Since many errors occur at boundary limits, BVA helps catch these off-by-one errors effectively.Boundary Value Analysis is based on testing the boundary values of valid and invalid partitions.

The behavior at the edge of the equivalence partition is more likely to be incorrect than the behavior within the partition, so boundaries are an area where testing is likely to yield defects.It checks for the input values near the boundary that have a higher chance of error. Every partition has its maximum and minimum values and these maximum and minimum values are the boundary values of a partition.

Note:

How Boundary Value Analysis Works

- Identify the input range or condition.
- Determine the boundary values.
- Test at and around the boundary (min, max, just below, just above).

Example: Consider a system that accepts ages from 18 to 56.

Boundary Value Analysis (Age accepts 18 to 56		
Invalid (min - 1)	Valid (min, min +1, nominal, max - 1, max)	Invalid (max + 1)
17	18, 19, 37, 55, 56	57

Valid Test cases: Valid test cases for the above can be any value entered greater than 17 and less than 57.

- Enter the value- 18.
- Enter the value- 19.
- Enter the value- 37.
- Enter the value- 55.
- Enter the value- 56.

Invalid Testcases: When any value less than 18 and greater than 56 is entered.

- Enter the value- 17.
- Enter the value- 57.

Single Fault Assumption: When more than one variable for the same application is checked then one can use a single fault assumption. Holding all but one variable to the extreme value and allowing the remaining variable to take the extreme value.

Advantages of Boundary Value Analysis

- Catches off-by-one and edge case errors.
- Covers common real-world issues (e.g., wrong loop conditions, overflow errors).
- Works well with Equivalence Partitioning to improve test efficiency.

Disadvantages of Boundary Value Analysis

- Does not test all inputs within a range.
- Might miss complex logical errors inside the code.

When to Use Boundary Value Analysis?

- When testing numeric input fields (age, salary, score, etc.).
- When dealing with range-based conditions (date limits, form validation, etc.).
- When you suspect bugs near the limits (edge cases).

Difference Between BVA and Equivalence Partitioning

Feature	Equivalence Partitioning	Boundary Value Analysis
Test Cases	Representative values from each partition	Tests extreme values at boundaries
Goal	Reduce test cases while covering all partitions	Catch errors at min/max limits

White Box Testing

White box testing is a Software Testing Technique that involves testing the internal structure and workings of a Software Application. The tester has access to the source code and uses this knowledge to design test cases that can verify the correctness of the software at the code level. White box testing is also known as Structural Testing or Code-based Testing, and it is used to test the software's internal logic, flow, and structure. The tester creates test cases to examine the code paths and logic flows to ensure they meet the specified requirements.

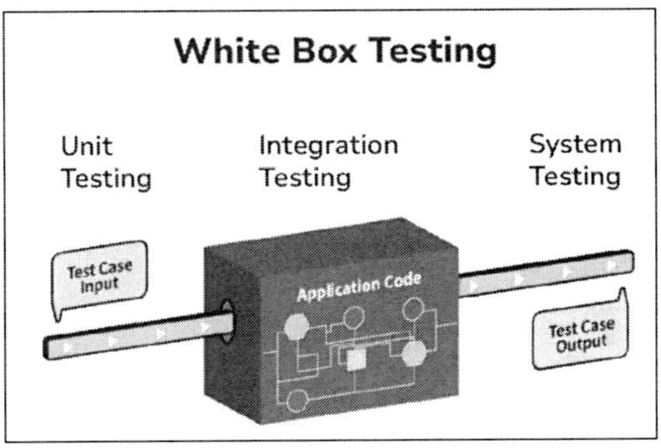

Figure 4.6

White box testing include testing a software application with an extend understanding of its internal code and structure. This type of testing allows testers to create detailed test cases based on the application's design and functionality.

Types Of White Box Testing

White box testing can be done for different purposes at different places. There are three main types of White Box testing which is follows:

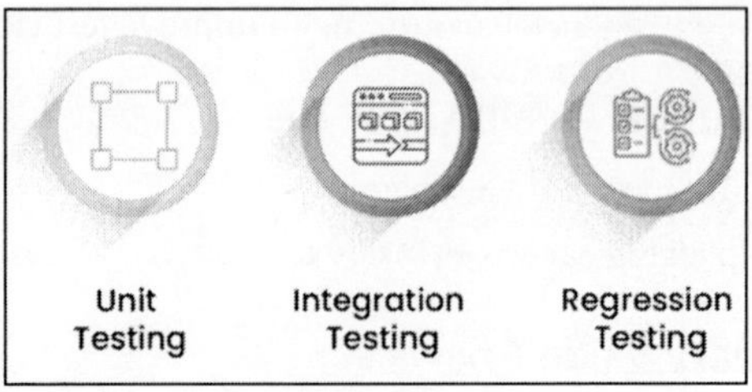

Figure 4.7

- **Unit Testing:** Unit Testing checks if each part or function of the application works correctly. It will check the application meets design requirements during development.
- **IntegrationTesting:** Integration Testing Examines how different parts of the application work together. After unit testing to make sure components work well both alone and together.
- **Regression Testing**: Regression Testing Verifies that changes or updates don't break existing functionality of the code. It will check the application still passes all existing tests after updates.

White Box Testing Techniques

One of the main benefits of white box testing is that it allows for testing every part of an application. To achieve complete code coverage, white box testing uses the following techniques.

Basis Path Testing & Data Flow Testing

Prerequisite: Path Testing Basis Path Testing is a white-box testing technique based on the control structure of a program or a module. Using this structure, a control flow graph is prepared and the various possible paths present in the graph are executed as a part of testing. Therefore, by definition, Basis path testing is a technique of selecting the paths in the control flow graph, that provide a basis set of execution paths through the program or module.

To design test cases using this technique, four steps are followed:

- Construct the Control Flow Graph
- Compute the Cyclomatic Complexity of the Graph
- Identify the Independent Paths
- Design Test cases from Independent Paths

Let's understand each step one by one.

1. Control Flow Graph – A control flow graph (or simply, flow graph) is a directed graph which represents the control structure of a program or module. A control flow graph (V, E) has V number of nodes/vertices and E number of edges in it. A control graph can also have:

- **Junction Node:** a node with more than one arrow entering it.
- **Decision Node:** a node with more than one arrow leaving it.
- **Region:** area bounded by edges and nodes (area outside the graph is also counted as a region.).

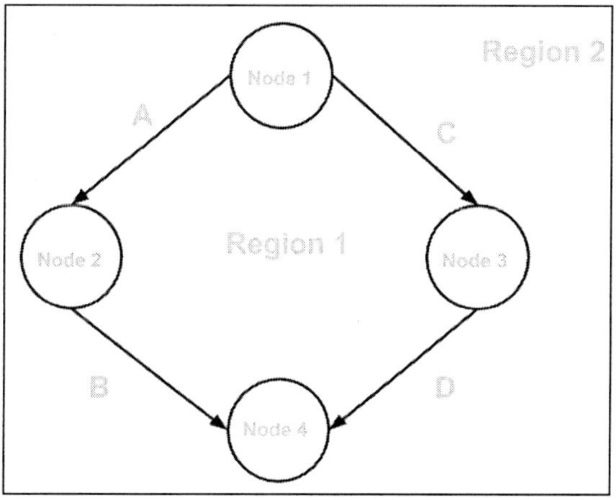

Figure 4.8

Below are the notations used while constructing a flow graph:

Sequential Statements

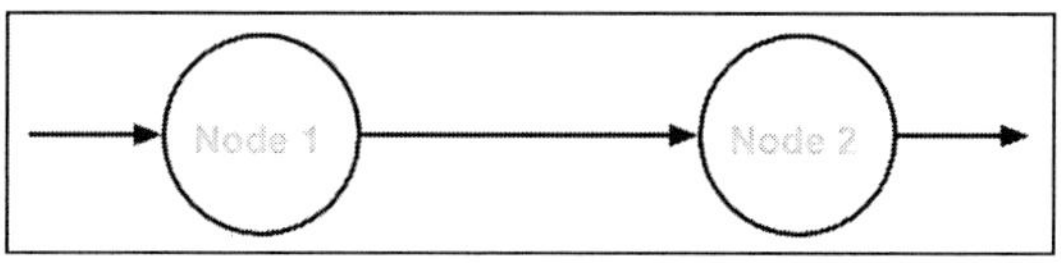

Figure 4.9 *Figure 4.10*

If – Then – Else

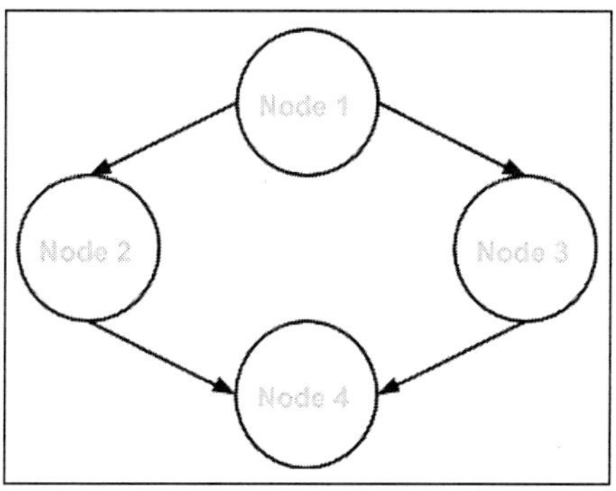

Figure 4.11

Do – While

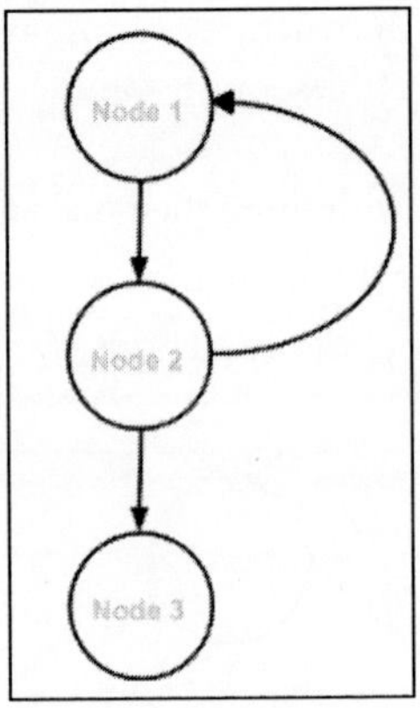

Figure 4.12

While – Do

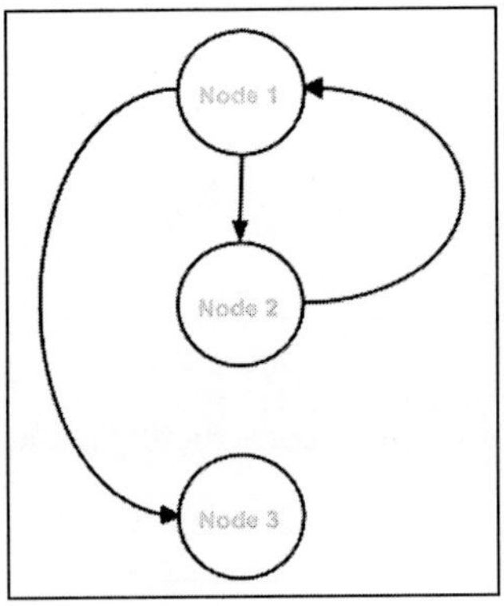

Figure 4.13, 14, 15

Switch – Case

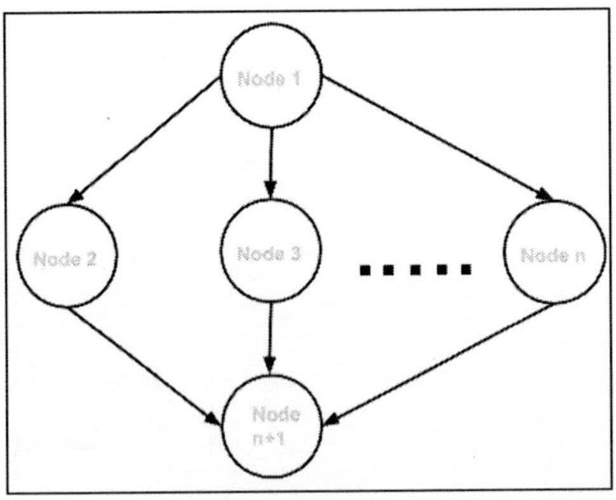

Figure 4.16

Cyclomatic Complexity: The cyclomatic complexity V(G) is said to be a measure of the logical complexity of a program. It can be calculated using three different formulae

Formula Based on edges and nodes

$$V(G) = e - n + 2*P$$

Where, e is number of edges, n is number of vertices, P is number of connected components. For example, consider first graph given above,

where, e = 4, n = 4 and p = 1

So,

Cyclomatic complexity V(G)

= 4 - 4 + 2 * 1

= 2

Formula Based on Decision Nodes

$$V(G) = d + P$$

where, d is number of decision nodes, P is number of connected nodes. For example, consider first graph given above,

where, d = 1 and p = 1

So,

Cyclomatic Complexity V(G) = 1 + 1= 2

Example: Basis Path Testing:

```
def check_number(x):
    if x > 0:
        print("Positive")
    elif x < 0:
        print("Negative")
    else:
        print("Zero")
```

Advantages of Basis Path Testing

- Ensures all logic paths are tested.
- Reduces redundant test cases.
- Helps find unreachable code & missing conditions.

Feature	Basis Path Testing	Data Flow Testing
Focus	Logical paths & control flow	Variable definitions & usage
Test Cases Based On	Cyclomatic Complexity & Paths	Variable tracking & data states
Detects	Unreachable code, missing conditions	Uninitialized variables, incorrect data propagation
Used In	Control-flow based testing	Data-driven code anslysis

Difference Between Basis Path Testing & Data Flow Testing

Data Flow Testing (DFT)

Data Flow Testing (DFT) is another **white-box testing** method that focuses on how **variables** are defined, used, and propagated in a program.

Key Objectives

- Ensure all **variables are properly initialized before use.**
- Detect **unused variables** or **unnecessary computations.**
- Prevent **uninitialized memory access or data leakage.**

Data Flow Mechanisms & Test Coverage Criteria

1. Define-Use Testing (DU-Testing)

- Ensures every **defined variable is used at least once.**
- Helps find **uninitialized variables.**

2. Use-Definition Chain Testing (UD-Chain)

- Tracks where a variable is **defined** and where it is **used.**
- Ensures correct data propagation.

3. All-Path Coverage

- Ensures every **execution path of a variable** is tested.

Example: Data Flow Testing

Aspect	Basis Path Testing	Data Flow Testing
Focus	Adherence to design standards	Creating a high-quality product design
Measurement	Consistency in production	Innovation, features, and specifications
Objective	Minimize defects & variations	Maximize functionality & user experience
Example	A smartphone's hardware being identical in all units	Designing a smartphone with advanced features

Checkpoints

- Is area used after being defined? (Yes)
- Are there any unused variables? (No)
- Are variables properly initialized? (Yes)

Advantages of Data Flow Testing

- Detects variable misuse & data leaks.
- Prevents memory issues (e.g., uninitialized variables).
- Helps optimize variable usage & memory efficiency.

When to Use Basis Path Testing & Data Flow Testing?

- Use Basis Path Testing when verifying code logic and control flow.
- Use Data Flow Testing when checking variable states, data usage, and propagation.
- Combine both to achieve maximum test coverage and efficiency.

4.3 Regression Testing

Regression testing is a crucial aspect of software engineering that ensures the stability and reliability of a software product. It involves retesting the previously tested functionalities to verify that recent code changes haven't adversely affected the existing features.

By identifying and fixing any regression or unintended bugs, regression testing helps maintain the overall quality of the software. This process is essential for software development teams to deliver consistent and high-quality products to their users.

4.3.1 What is Regression Testing?

Regression testing is like a software quality checkup after any changes are made. It involves running tests to make sure that everything still works as it should, even after updates or tweaks to the code. This ensures that the software remains reliable and functions properly, maintaining its integrity throughout its development lifecycle.

When to Do regression testing?

When new functionality is added to the system and the code has been modified to absorb and integrate that functionality with the existing code. When some defect has been identified in the software and the code is debugged to fix it. When the code is modified to optimize its working.

Process of Regression Testing

Firstly, whenever we make some changes to the source code for any reason like adding new functionality, optimization, etc. then our program when executed fails in the previously designed test suite for obvious reasons. After the failure, the source code is debugged to identify the bugs in the program.

After identification of the bugs in the source code, appropriate modifications are made. Then appropriate test cases are selected from the already existing test suite which covers all the modified and affected parts of the source code. We can add new test cases if required. In the end, regression testing is performed using the selected test cases.

Techniques for the Selection of Test cases for Regression Testing

- **Select all test cases:** In this technique, all the test cases are selected from the already existing test suite. It is the simplest and safest technique but not very efficient.
- **Select test cases randomly:** In this technique, test cases are selected randomly from the existing test suite, but it is only useful if all the test cases are equally good in their fault detection capability which is very rare. Hence, it is not used in most of the cases.
- **Select modification traversing test cases:** In this technique, only those test cases are selected that cover and test the modified portions of the source code and the parts that are affected by these modifications.

- **Select higher priority test cases**: In this technique, priority codes are assigned to each test case of the test suite based upon their bug detection capability, customer requirements, etc. After assigning the priority codes, test cases with the highest priorities are selected for the process of regression testing. The test case with the highest priority has the highest rank. For example, a test case with priority code 2 is less important than a test case with priority code 1.

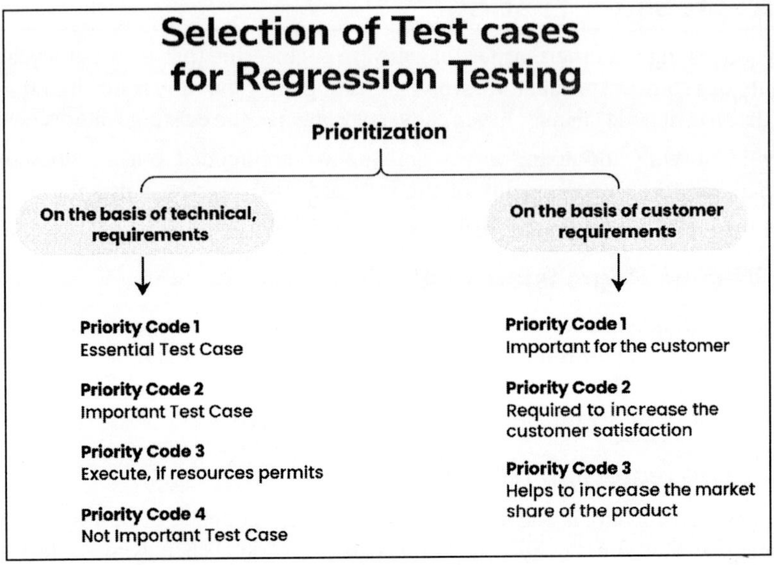

Figure 4.14

Top Regression Testing Tools In regression testing, we generally select the test cases from the existing test suite itself and hence, we need not compute their expected output, and it can be easily automated due to this reason. Automating the process of regression testing will be very effective and time-saving.

Advantages of Regression Testing

- Automated unit testing
- Comprehensive test coverage
- System integration
- Faster test execution completion
- Improved developer productivity
- Parallel testing
- Reduced costs

Disadvantages of Regression Testing

- It can be time and resource-consuming if automated tools are not used.
- It is required even after very small changes in the code.
- Time and Resource Constraints.
- Among the significant risks associated with regression testing are the time and resources required to perform it.

- Incomplete or Insufficient Test Coverage.
- False Positives and False Negatives.
- Test Data Management Challenges.

Conclusion

Regression testing is like a safety net for software changes, making sure they do not bring in new problems. It picks test cases from existing suites, sometimes focusing on modified parts. Popular tools like Selenium and QTP automate this process. While it ensures thorough testing, doing it manually can up time and encounter data management issues.

4.4 Levels of Testing

Software Testing is an activity performed to identify errors so that errors can be removed to obtain a product with greater quality. To assure and maintain the quality of software and to represent the ultimate review of specification, design, and coding, Software testing is required. There are different levels of testing.Software testing is performed in different **levels** to ensure **each part of the application functions correctly** before moving to the next stage.

Four Main Levels of Testing

- **Unit Testing** 🧩 (Tests individual components)
- **Integration Testing** 🔗 (Tests connections between components)
- **System Testing** 💻 (Tests the entire application)
- **Acceptance Testing**• (Tests if the system meets user requirements)

1. Unit Testing

In this type of testing, errors are detected individually from every component or unit by individually testing the components or units of software to ensure that they are fit for use by the developers. It is the smallest testable part of the software.

Who performs it?

- **Developers** (using frameworks like JUnit, PyTest, NUnit).

Example

```
def add(a, b):
    return a + b


def test_add():
    assert add(2, 3) == 5  # ✅ Pass
    assert add(-1, 1) == 0  # ✅ Pass
```

Why?

- Catches bugs **early in development**.
- Improves **code quality and reliability**.

Tools

- **JUnit** (Java), **PyTest** (Python), **NUnit** (C#), **Google Test** (C++)

2. Integration Testing

In this testing, two or more modules which are unit tested are integrated to test i.e., technique interacting components, and are then verified if these integrated modules work as per the expectation or not, and interface errors are also detected.

Types of Integration Testing

- **Top-down** 📍 (Start with high-level modules → lower-level ones)
- **Bottom-up** 🔽 (Start with lower-level modules → higher-level ones)
- **Big Bang** 💥 (Test all modules together at once)
- **Incremental** 🔄 (Test module by module)

Example

- Testing **Login + Database interaction**:
- **Login Module** sends **username & password**.
- **Database Module** validates credentials.
- The system should return **"Login Successful" or "Invalid Credentials"**.

Why?

- Ensures **modules work together correctly**.
- Detects **data mismatches, communication issues**.

Tools

- **Postman** (API Testing), **JUnit**, **TestNG**, **Selenium**

3. System Testing

In system testing, complete and integrated Software's are tested i.e., all the system elements forming the system are tested as a whole to meet the requirements of the system.

Types of System Testing

- **Functional Testing** (Checks system behavior)
- **Performance Testing** (Speed & scalability)
- **Security Testing** (Detects vulnerabilities)
- **Usability Testing** (Checks user-friendliness)

Example

- **E-commerce System Test**:
  - **Search for a product** → Should return correct results.
  - **Add to Cart** → Should update cart count.
  - **Checkout & Payment** → Should process payments correctly.

Why?

- Ensures the **entire system works correctly**.
- Validates **business requirements & specifications.**

Tools

- **Selenium**, **LoadRunner** (Performance Testing), **JMeter**

4. Acceptance Testing

This is a kind of testing conducted to ensure that the requirements of the users are fulfilled before its delivery and that the software works correctly in the user's working environment.

Types of Acceptance Testing

- **User Acceptance Testing (UAT):** Performed by **end-users.**
- **Business Acceptance Testing (BAT):** Ensures business goals are met.
- **Regulatory Testing:** Checks compliance with legal standards.

Example

- **Banking App UAT Test Case:**
  - **User logs in** → Sees account balance.
  - **Transfers money** → Receives confirmation message.
  - **Logs out** → Redirected to login page.

Why?

- Determines if the **software is ready for deployment.**
- Ensures it **meets user expectations.**

Tools

- **TestRail** (Test case management), **Selenium**, **JIRA** (Bug tracking)

Summary: Levels of Testing

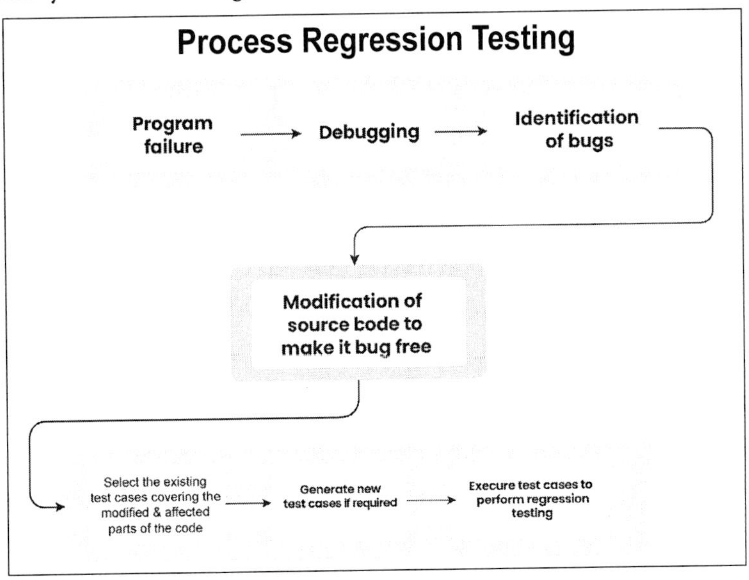

Figure 4.15

These tests can be conducted at various stages of software development. The levels of testing along with the corresponding software development phase are shown in the following diagram:

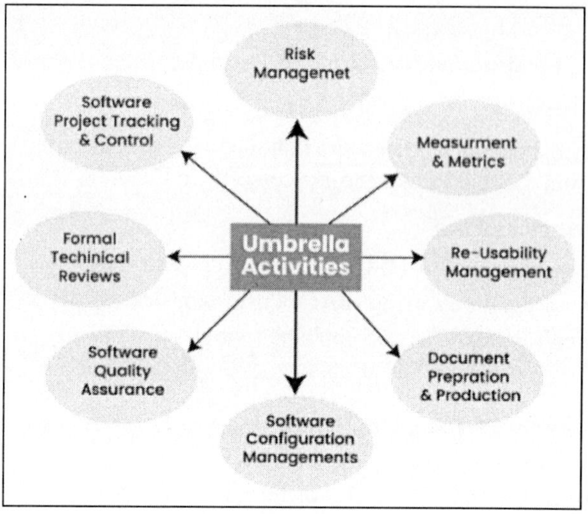

Figure 4.16

The requirements of customers should be traceable and identified by all different tests. Planning of tests that how tests will be conducted should be done long before the beginning of the test. The Pareto principle can be applied to software testing- 80% of all errors identified during testing will likely be traceable to 20% of all program modules. Testing should begin "in the small" and progress toward testing "in the large". Exhaustive testing which simply means to test all the possible combinations of data is not possible.

Unit Testing – Software Testing

Unit Testing is a software testing technique in which individual units or components of a software application are tested in isolation. These units are the smallest pieces of code, typically functions or methods, ensuring they perform as expected. Unit testing helps in identifying bugs early in the development cycle, enhancing code quality, and reducing the cost of fixing issues later. It is an essential part of Test-Driven Development (TDD), promoting reliable code.

What is Unit Testing?

Unit testing is the process of testing the smallest parts of your code, like individual functions or methods, to make sure they work correctly. It's a key part of software development that improves code quality by testing each unit in isolation. You write unit tests for these code units and run them automatically every time you make changes.

If a test fails, it helps you quickly find and fix the issue. Unit testing promotes modular code, ensures better test coverage, and saves time by allowing developers to focus more on coding than manual testing.A unit test is a small piece of code that checks if a specific function or method in is an application works correctly. It will work as the function inputs and verifying the outputs. These tests check that the code work as expected based on the logic the developer intended.

Unit Testing Strategies

To create effective **unit tests**, follow these basic techniques to ensure all scenarios are covered:

- **Logic checks**: Verify if the system performs correct calculations and follows the expected path with valid inputs. Check all possible paths through the code are tested.
- **Boundary checks**: Test how the system handles typical, edge case, and invalid inputs. For example, if an integer between 3 and 7 is expected, check how the system reacts to a 5 (normal), a 3 (edge case), and a 9 (invalid input).
- **Error handling**: Check the system properly handles errors. Does it prompt for a new input, or does it crash when something goes wrong?
- **Object-oriented checks:** If the code modifies objects, confirm that the object's state is correctly updated after running the code.

How do Developers Use Unit Tests

Unit testing plays an important role throughout the software development process:

- **Test-Driven Development (TDD):** In **TDD**, developers write tests before writing the actual code. This ensures that once the code is completed, it instantly meets the functional requirements when tested, saving time on debugging.
- **After Completing Code Blocks:** After a section of code is finished, unit tests are created (if not already done through TDD). These tests are then run to verify that the code works as expected. Unit tests are rarely the first set of tests run during broader system testing.
- **DevOps and CI/CD:** In DevOps environments, Continuous Integration/ Continuous Delivery (CI/CD) automatically runs unit tests whenever new code is added. This ensures that changes are integrated smoothly, tested thoroughly, and deployed efficiently, maintaining overall code quality.

Unit Test Example

```
import static org.junit.jupiter.api.Assertions.assertEquals;
import org.junit.jupiter.api.Test;

public class CalculatorTest {

    @Test
    public void testAddPositives() {
        int result = Calculator.addTwoNumbers(5, 40);
        assertEquals(45, result);
    }

    @Test
    public void testAddNegatives() {
        int result = Calculator.addTwoNumbers(-4, -50);
        assertEquals(-54, result);
    }
```

```
    @Test
    public void testAddMixed() {
        int result = Calculator.addTwoNumbers(5, -5);
        assertEquals(0, result);
    }
}
```

When is Unit Testing Less Beneficial?

Unit testing is not always necessary for every piece of code in every project. Here are some situations where it might be okay to skip unit tests:

- **Time Constraints:** Writing unit tests can take a lot of time, even with automated tools. If your team is under pressure, they might get distract while writing tests and miss deadlines, leading to budget issues.
- **UI/UX Focus:** If the main focus of the application is on design and user experience rather than complex logic, manual testing might be more effective than unit testing.
- **Legacy Code:** Testing old or legacy code can be very challenging. If the existing code is not written well then it may be hard to add tests without reference writing, which can be time-consuming.
- **Changing Requirements:** In projects where requirements are frequently changing, it may not be practical to write tests for all code, as the code may change before the tests are even run.

Types of Unit Testing

There are two types of Unit testing methods:

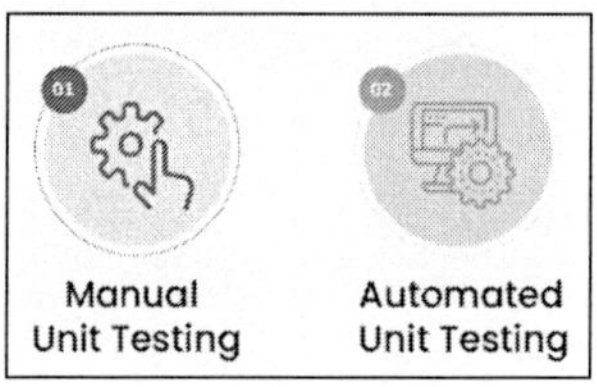

Figure 4.17

Manual Testing

Manual testing is like checking each part of a project by hand, without using any special tools. People, like developers, do each step of the testing themselves. But manual unit testing isn't used much because there are better ways to do it and it has some problems:

- It costs more because workers have to be paid for the time they spend testing, especially if they're not permanent staff.
- It takes a lot of time because tests have to be done every time the code changes.
- It is hard to find and fix problems because it is tricky to test each part separately.
- Developers often do manual testing themselves to see if their code works correctly.

Automated Unit Testing

Automated unit testing is a way of checking if software works correctly without needing lots of human effort. We use special tools made by people to run these tests automatically.

These are part of the process of building the software. Here's how it works:

- Developers write a small piece of code to test a function in the software. This code is like a little experiment to see if everything works as it should.
- Before the software is finished and sent out to users, these test codes are taken out. They're only there to make sure everything is working properly during development.

Workflow of Unit Testing

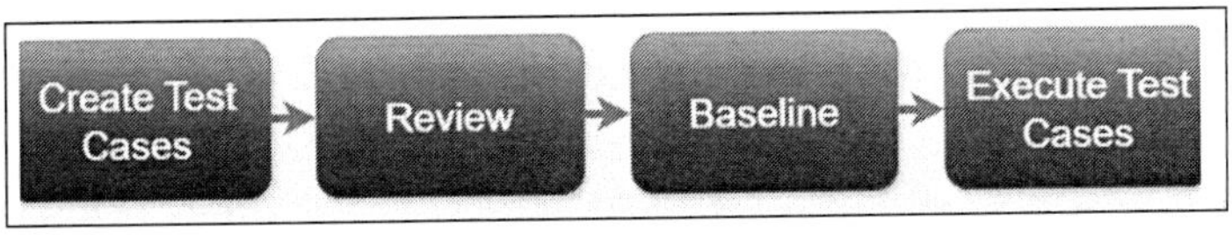

Figure 4.18

Unit Testing Techniques

There are 3 types of Unit Testing Techniques. They are follows

- **Black Box Testing:** This testing technique is used in covering the unit tests for input, user interface, and output parts.
- **White Box Testing:** This technique is used in testing the functional behavior of the system by giving the input and checking the functionality output including the internal design structure and code of the modules.
- **Gray Box Testing:** This technique is used in executing the relevant test cases, test methods, and test functions, and analyzing the code performance for the modules.

Unit testing will validate individual units of software in a proper manner, checking if the function works correctly and meets the requirements of the project. While it may offer benefits such as early issue detection and improved code quality, it requires significant time and effort, which depends on the developers' skills.

Integration Testing – Software Engineering

Integration testing is the process of testing the interface between two software units or modules. It focuses on determining the correctness of the interface. The purpose of integration testing is to expose faults in the interaction between integrated units. Once all the modules have been unit-tested, integration testing is performed.

What is Integration Testing?

Integration testing is a software testing technique that focuses on verifying the interactions and data exchange between different components or modules of a software application. The goal of integration testing is to identify any problems or bugs that arise when different components are combined and interact with each other. Integration testing is typically performed after unit testing and before system testing.

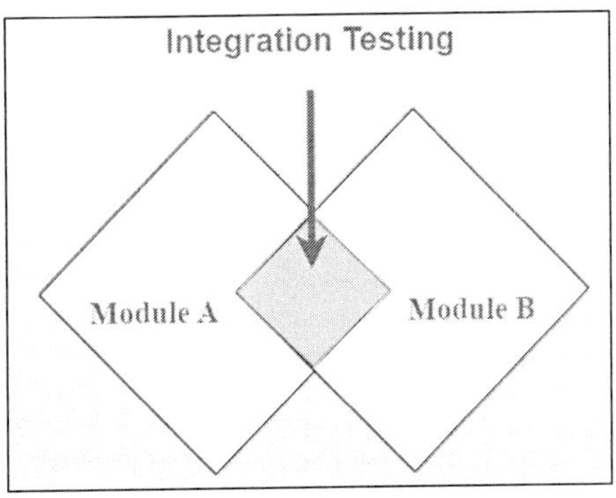

Figure 4.19

- Integration testing can be done by picking module by module.
- This can be done so that there should be a proper sequence to be followed. And also, if you don't want to miss out on any integration scenarios then you have to follow the proper sequence.
- Exposing the defects is the major focus of the integration testing and the time of interaction between the integrated units.

Why is Integration Testing Important?

Integration testing is important because it verifies that individual software modules or components work together correctly as a whole system. This ensures that the integrated software functions as intended and helps identify any compatibility or communication issues between different parts of the system. By detecting and resolving integration problems early, integration testing contributes to the overall reliability, performance, and quality of the software product.

Integration Test Approaches There are Four Types of Integration Testing Approaches

1. Big-Bang Integration Testing

It is the simplest integration testing approach, where all the modules are combined and the functionality is verified after the completion of individual module testing.

In simple words, all the modules of the system are simply put together and tested. This approach is practicable only for very small systems. If an error is found during the integration testing, it is very difficult to localize the error as the error may potentially belong to any of the modules being integrated.

So, debugging errors reported during Big Bang integration testing is very expensive to fix. Big-bang integration testing is a software testing approach in which all components or modules of a software application are combined and tested at once. Those approaches are the following:

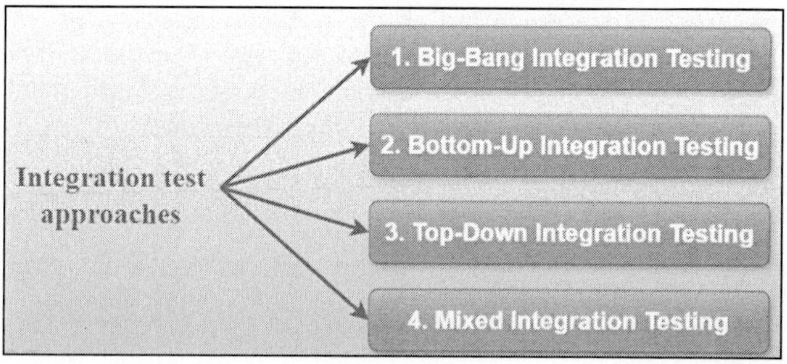

Figure 4.20

2. Bottom-Up Integration Testing

In bottom-up testing, each module at lower levels are tested with higher modules until all modules are tested. The primary purpose of this integration testing is that each subsystem tests the interfaces among various modules making up the subsystem. This integration testing uses test drivers to drive and pass appropriate data to the lower-level modules.

3. Top-Down Integration Testing

Top-down integration testing technique is used in order to simulate the behaviour of the lower-level modules that are not yet integrated. In this integration testing, testing takes place from top to bottom. First, high-level modules are tested and then low-level modules and finally integrating the low-level modules to a high level to ensure the system is working as intended.

4. Mixed Integration Testing

A mixed integration testing is also called sandwiched integration testing. A mixed integration testing follows a combination of top down and bottom-up testing approaches. In top-down approach, testing can start only after the top-level module have been coded and unit tested. In bottom-up approach, testing can start only after the bottom level modules are ready. This sandwich or mixed approach overcomes this shortcoming of the top-down and bottom-up approaches. It is also called the hybrid integration testing. also, stubs and drivers are used in mixed integration testing.

Example 1: API Integration Test (Postman)

Scenario

- A **Weather App** fetches data from an **External Weather API**.

Test Case

- Send a **GET request** to https://api.weather.com/current?city=NewYork.
- Validate **response format & status code (200 OK)**.
- Ensure **correct temperature data is returned**.

Why?

- Ensures the app **correctly fetches and displays weather data**.

Integration testing is a critical phase in software development that ensures all components work together seamlessly. Various approaches like Big-Bang, Bottom-Up, Top-Down, and Mixed Integration Testing help validate the integration points and interactions between modules. Each approach has its advantages and disadvantages, catering to different project needs. Proper integration testing helps identify defects early, ensuring the reliability, performance, and quality of the software product.

Integration Testing vs. Unit Testing

Feature	Unit Testing	Integration Testing
Scope	Individual function/module	Multiple interacting modules
Focus	Internal logic of a single function	Data flow & communication between modules
Who Performs?	Developers	Developers & Testers
Example	Testing add(a, b) function	Testing Login Module with Database
Automation?	Often automated	Patially automated

System Testing – Software Engineering

System Testing is a **high-level software testing process** where the **entire application** is tested as a complete system to ensure it meets all functional and non-functional requirements.

System testing is a type of software testing that evaluates the overall functionality and performance of a complete and fully integrated software solution. It tests if the system meets the specified requirements and if it is suitable for delivery to the end-users. This type of testing is performed after the integration testing and before the acceptance testing.

What is System Testing?

System Testing is a type of software testing_that is performed on a completely integrated system to evaluate the compliance of the system with the corresponding requirements. In system testing, integration testing passed components are taken as input.

- The goal of integration testing is to detect any irregularity between the units that are integrated. System testing detects defects within both the integrated units and the whole system. The result of system testing is the observed behaviour of a component or a system when it is tested.
- **System Testing** is carried out on the whole system in the context of either system requirement specifications or functional requirement specifications or the context of both. System testing tests the design and behaviour of the system and also the expectations of the customer.
- It is performed to test the system beyond the bounds mentioned in the software requirements specification (SRS) . System Testing is performed by a testing team that is independent of the development team and helps to test the quality of the system impartial.
- It has both functional and non-functional testing. System Testing is a black-box testing. System Testing is performed after the integration testing and before the acceptance testing.

System testing is evergreen role in software engineering because every software is needed to test and very update is needed to test so the demand of the software tester is always needed. If you wish to learn software testing from the scratch and want to grab a good grip on testing tools and concept you can check our new software testing course.

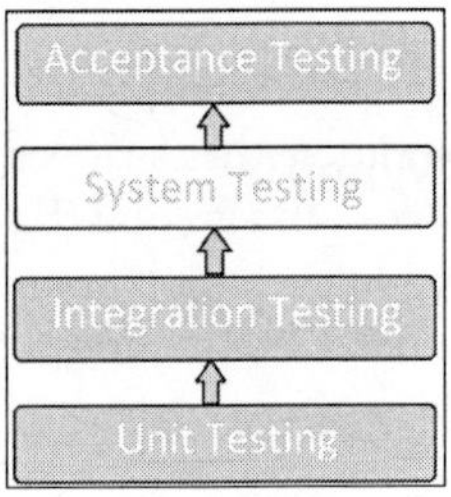

Figure 4.21

System Testing Process

System Testing is performed in the following steps:

- **Test Environment Setup:** Create testing environment for the betterquality testing.
- **Create Test Case:** Generate test case for the testing process.
- **Create Test Data:** Generate the data that is to be tested.
- **Execute Test Case:** After the generation of the test case and the test data, test cases are executed.
- **Defect Reporting:** Defects in the system are detected.
- **Regression Testing:** It is carried out to test the side effects of the testing process.
- **Log Defects:** Defects are fixed in this step.

- **Retest:** If the test is not successful then again test is performed.

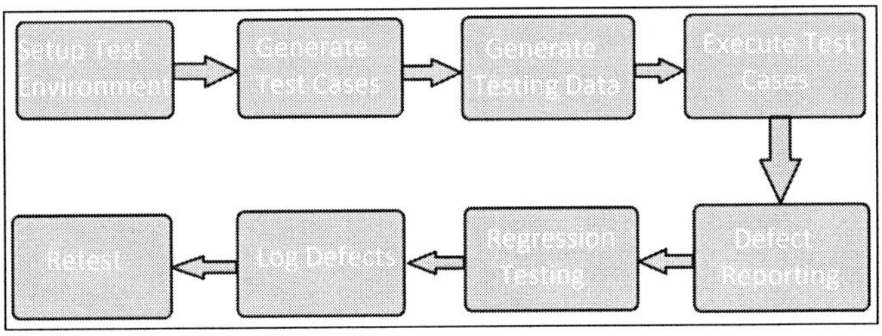

Figure 4.22

Types of System Testing

- **Performance Testing:** Performance Testing is a type of software testing that is carried out to test the speed, scalability, stability and reliability of the software product or application.
- **Load Testing:** Load Testing is a type of software Testing which is carried out to determine the behavior of a system or software product under extreme load.
- **Stress Testing:** Stress Testing is a type of software testing performed to check the robustness of the system under the varying loads.
- **Scalability Testing:** Scalability Testing is a type of software testing which is carried out to check the performance of a software application or system in terms of its capability to scale up or scale down the number of user request load.

Why is System Testing Important?

- Ensures the entire system works as expected.
- Validates functional, performance, security, and usability aspects.
- Identifies bugs that may arise when integrating modules.
- Mimics real-world usage before deployment.

Who Performs System Testing?

- **QA Engineers/Testers:** Conduct system-level tests.
- **Developers:** Assist with debugging system-wide issues.
- **End-Users (Beta Testers):** Perform User Acceptance Testing (UAT).

Example of System Testing

Scenario: Testing an E-commerce Website

Test Cases

- **Login Page Test:** Enter valid & invalid credentials.
- **Product Search Test:** Search for items and check results.
- **Add to Cart Test:** Add items and verify prices.
- **Payment Gateway Test:** Ensure payments are processed securely.
- **Page Load Speed Test:** Ensure pages load within 2 seconds.
- **Mobile Compatibility Test:** Check functionality on iOS & Android.

Feature	Unit Testing	Integration Testing	System Testing
Scope	Single function/module	Module interactions	Whole system
Performed By	Developers	Developers & Testers	QA Engineers
Focus	Code correctness	Data flow between modules	Real-world behavior
Example	Testing login() function	Testing Login & Databse	Testing full e-commerce platform

System Testing Best Practices

- Test real-world user scenarios (end-to-end testing).
- Perform security and performance testing early.
- Automate repetitive tests using tools like Selenium, JMeter, Appium.
- Use cloud-based testing environments for broader compatibility.

Acceptance Testing – Software Testing

Acceptance Testing is the **final phase of software testing** before release. It **validates** whether the software meets the **business requirements** and is ready for deployment.

Acceptance Testing is an important aspect of Software Testing, which guarantees that software aligns with user needs and business requirements. The major aim of this test is to evaluate the compliance of the system with the business requirements and assess whether it is acceptable for delivery or not.

What is Acceptance Testing?

It is formal testing according to user needs, requirements, and business processes conducted to determine whether a system satisfies the acceptance criteria or not and to enable the users, customers, or other authorized entities to determine whether to accept the system or not. Acceptance Testing is the last phase of software testing performed after System Testing and before making the system available for actual use.

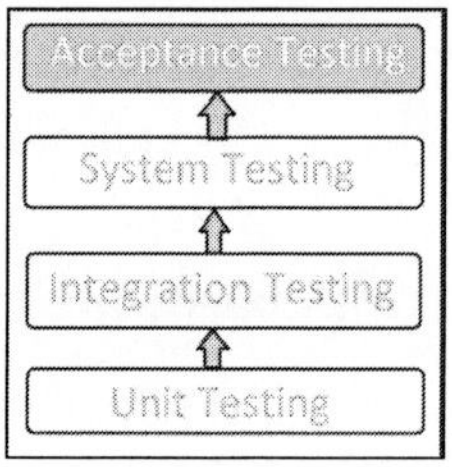

Figure 4.23

Why is Acceptance Testing Important?

- Ensures the software fulfils business & customer expectations.
- Reduces the risk of failures after deployment.
- Increases stakeholder confidence in the product.
- Identifies bugs and usability issues before release.

Types of Acceptance Testing

Here are the types of Acceptance Testing:

1. User Acceptance Testing (UAT)

- User acceptance testing is used to determine whether the product is working for the user correctly.

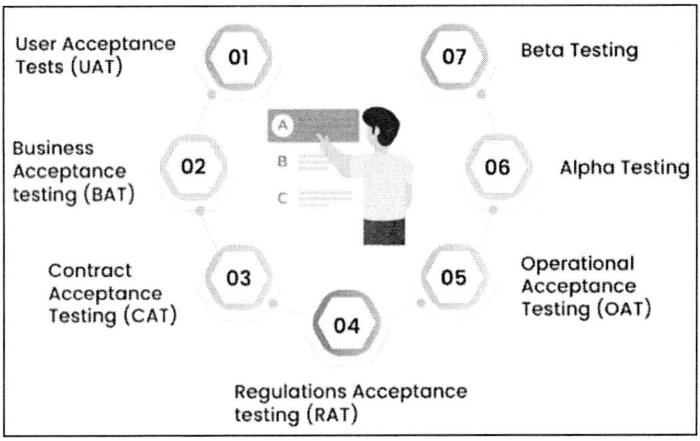

Figure 4.24

- Specific requirements which are quite often used by the customers are primarily picked for testing purposes. This is also termed as End-User Testing.

2. Business Acceptance Testing (BAT)

- BAT is used to determine whether the product meets the business goals and purposes or not.
- BAT mainly focuses on business profits which are quite challenging due to the changing market conditions and new technologies, so the current implementation may have to being changed which results in extra budgets.

3. Contract Acceptance Testing (CAT)

- CAT is a contract that specifies that once the product goes live, within a predetermined period, the acceptance test must be performed, and it should pass all the acceptance use cases.
- Here is a contract termed a Service Level Agreement (SLA), which includes the terms where the payment will be made only if the Product services are in-line with all the requirements, which means the contract is fulfilled.

4. Regulations Acceptance Testing (RAT)

- RAT is used to determine whether the product violates the rules and regulations that are defined by the government of the country where it is being released.
- This may be unintentional but will impact negatively on the business. Generally, the product or application that is to be released in the market, has to go under RAT, as different countries or regions have different rules and regulations defined by its governing bodies.
- If any rules and regulations are violated for any country then that country or the specific region then the product will not be released in that country or region.

5. Operational Acceptance Testing (OAT)

- OAT is used to determine the operational readiness of the product and is non-functional testing.

- It mainly includes testing of recovery, compatibility, maintainability, reliability, etc. OAT assures the stability of the product before it is released to production.

6. Alpha Testing

- Alpha testing is used to determine the product in the development testing environment by a specialized testers team usually called alpha testers.

7. Beta Testing

- Beta testing is used to assess the product by exposing it to the real end-users, typically called beta testers in their environment.
- Feedback is collected from the users and the defects are fixed. Also, this helps in enhancing the product to give a rich user experience.

Use of Acceptance Testing

- To find the defects missed during the functional testing phase.
- How well the product is developed.
- A product is what actually the customers need.
- Feedback help in improving the product performance and user experience.
- Minimize or eliminate the issues arising from the production.

Who Performs Acceptance Testing?

- End Users (Customers, Clients, Business Analysts, Product Owners)
- QA Teams & Testers
- Stakeholders & Management

Example of Acceptance Testing

Scenario: UAT for an Online Banking App

Test Cases

- **Login Test:** Verify users can log in with valid credentials.
- Fund Transfer Test: Check if money transfer between accounts works.
- Bill Payment Test: Ensure users can pay utility bills.
- Mobile App Test: Confirm smooth usage on Android & iOS.
- Security Test: Verify OTP authentication & encryption.

Best Practices for Acceptance Testing

- Define clear acceptance criteria with stakeholders.
- Involve real end-users for practical feedback.
- Test in a real-world production-like environment.
- Automate repetitive acceptance tests for efficiency.
- Ensure regulatory compliance (GDPR, HIPAA, etc.).

Acceptance Testing vs Other Testing Types

Acceptance testing ensures software meets user needs and business requirements. It includes types like UAT, BAT, CAT, RAT, OAT, Alpha, and Beta testing. While involving users directly, it faces challenges like user participation and time-consuming feedback collection.

Feature	System Testing	Acceptance Testing
Scope	Tests the entire system	Tests if the system meets business needs
Performed By	QA engineers	End users, stakeholders
Focus	Functionality, performance, security	Business goals, real-world usability
Example	Checking if login works technically	Checking if login is easy for customers

Difference Between Unit, Integration, System, and Acceptance Testing

Feature	Unit Testing	Integration Testing	System Testing	Acceptance Testing
Purpose	Tests individual components or functions.	Tests interactions between integrated modules.	Tests the entire system as a whole.	Validates if the software meets business and user requirements.
Performed By	Developers	Developers & Testers	QA Testers	End-users, stakeholders, clients
Scope	A single function/module	Multiple connected modules	The complete system	Real-world user scenarios
Example	Testing a `login()` function separately.	Checking if the ↓ login module	Testing the full e-commerce website	Ensuring customers can easily place

Final Thought

- Unit Testing ensures each function works correctly.
- Integration Testing ensures modules communicate properly.
- System Testing ensures the entire system functions as expected.
- Acceptance Testing ensures the software is ready for deployment.

Conclusion on Software Testing Software testing is a critical process in software development that ensures the reliability, functionality, security, and performance of an application before its release. By identifying defects early, testing helps reduce development costs, prevent failures, and improve user satisfaction. Different levels of testingunit, integration, system, and acceptance testingwork together to validate both individual components and the overall system.

Additionally, various testing approaches, such as black box, white box, and grey box testing, help ensure that software meets both technical and business requirements. With the rise of Agile and DevOps, continuous testing has become essential for delivering high-quality software at speed. Ultimately, a well-structured testing strategy enhances software quality, minimizes risks, and ensures a smooth user experience, making it an indispensable part of modern software development.

This page is intentionally left blank!

UMBRELLA ACTIVITIES & PROJECT MANAGEMENT AND ESTIMATION

5

UNIT

Umbrella Activities in Software Engineering

Software engineering is a collection of interconnected phlwases. These steps are expressed or available in different ways in different software process models. Umbrella activities, such as project management, quality assurance, and documentation, support these phases, ensuring consistency, quality, and efficient progress throughout the development process.

The activities in the software development process are supplemented by many general activities. Generally, common activities apply to the entire software project and help the software development team manage and track progress, quality, changes, and risks.

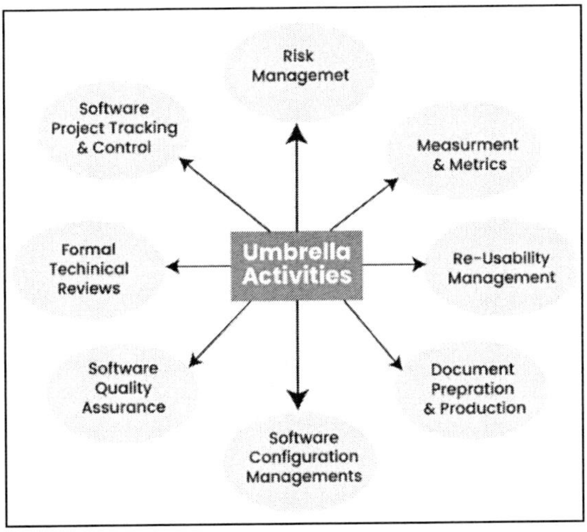

Figure 5.1

- **Software project tracking and control:** This activity allows the software team to check the progress of software development. Before the actual development starts, make a software development plan and develop on this basis, but after a certain period of time, it is necessary to analyze the development progress to find out what measures need to be taken. It must be accepted at an appropriate time after the completion of development, testing, etc. The test results may need to reschedule the development time.
- **Risk management:** Risk management is a series of steps to help software development teams understand and manage uncertainty. It is a very good idea to identify it, assess the likelihood of it happening, assess its impact, and develop an "if the problem does happen" contingency plan.

- **Software quality assurance**: As its name suggest this defines and conducts the activities required to ensure software quality. The quality of the software, such as user experience, performance, workload flexibility, etc., must be tested and verified after reaching the specified milestones, which reduces the tasks at the end of the development process, which must be performed by a dedicated team so that the development can continue.
- **Technical reviews:** It assesses software engineering work products in an effort to uncover and remove errors before they are propagated to the next activity. Software engineering is done in clusters or modules, after completing each module, it is good practice to review the completed module to find out and remove errors so their propagation to the next module can be prevented.
- **Measurement:** This includes all measurements of all aspects of the software project. Define and compile process, project, and product metrics to help the team deliver software that meets the needs of stakeholders; it can be used in conjunction with all other frameworks and general operations.
- **Software configuration management**: It manages the impact of changes throughout the software development process. Software Configuration Management (SCM) is a set of activities designed to manage changes by identifying work products that can be changed, establishing relationships between them, and defining mechanisms for managing different versions of them. Work product.
- **Reusability management:** Define the standards for the reuse of work products (including software components), and develop mechanisms to implement reusable components. This includes the approval of any part of a backing-up software project or any type of support provided for updates or updates in the future. Update the software according to user/current time requirements.
- **Work product preparation and production:** It encompasses the activities required to create work products such as models, documents, logs, forms, and lists.

Conclusion

Umbrella activities in software engineering provide essential support for the main development tasks. They ensure project management, quality assurance, and configuration control, maintaining consistency and quality. Documentation supports understanding and future maintenance. Overall, these activities enhance efficiency and reliability throughout the development process.

5.1 Risk Management

Risk management is the process of identifying, analyzing, and mitigating potential risks that could negatively impact a project's objectives. Effective risk management ensures project success by minimizing uncertainties and enhancing decision-making.

A risk is a probable problem; it might happen, or it might not. There are main two characteristics of risk.

- **Uncertainty:** the risk may or may not happen which means there are no 100% risks.
- **Loss:** If the risk occurs in reality, undesirable results or losses will occur.
- **What is Risk Management:** Risk Management is a systematic process of recognizing, evaluating, and handling threats or risks that have an effect on the

finances, capital, and overall operations of an organization. These risks can come from different areas, such as financial instability, legal issues, errors in strategic planning, accidents, and natural disasters.

- **Why is risk management important:** Risk management is important because it helps organizations to prepare for unexpected circumstances that can vary from small issues to major crises. By actively understanding, evaluating, and planning for potential risks, organizations can protect their financial health, continued operation, and overall survival.
- **The risk management process:** Risk management is a sequence of steps that help a software team to understand, analyze, and manage uncertainty. Risk management process consists of

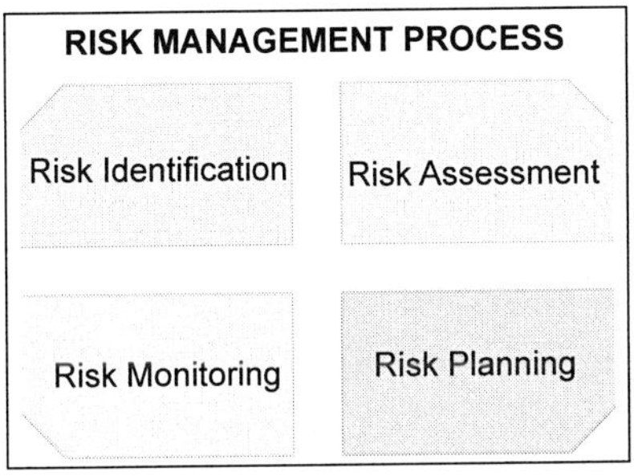

Figure 5.2

Risks Identification

Risk identification refers to the systematic process of recognizing and evaluating potential threats or hazards that could negatively impact an organization, its operations, or its workforce. This involves identifying various types of risks, ranging from IT security threats like viruses and phishing attacks to unforeseen events such as equipment failures and extreme weather conditions.

Risk analysis

Risk analysis is the process of evaluating and understanding the potential impact and likelihood of identified risks on an organization. It helps determine how serious a risk is and how to best manage or mitigate it. Risk Analysis involves evaluating each risk's probability and potential consequences to prioritize and manage them effectively.

Risk Planning

Risk planning involves developing strategies and actions to manage and mitigate identified risks effectively. It outlines how to respond to potential risks, including prevention, mitigation, and contingency measures, to protect the organization's objectives and assets.

Risk Monitoring

Risk monitoring involves continuously tracking and overseeing identified risks to assess their status, changes, and effectiveness of mitigation strategies. It ensures that risks are regularly reviewed and managed to maintain alignment with organizational objectives and adapt to new developments or challenges.

- **Understanding Risks in Software Projects:** A computer code project may be laid low with an outsized sort of risk. To be ready to consistently establish the necessary risks that could affect a computer code project, it's necessary to group risks into completely different categories. The project manager will then examine the risks from every category square measure relevant to the project.
- **Project risks**: concern various sorts of monetary funds, schedules, personnel, resources, and customer-related issues. A vital project risk is schedule slippage. Since computer code is intangible, it's tough to observe and manage a computer code project. It's tough to manage one thing that cannot be seen. For any producing project, like producing cars, the project manager will see the merchandise taking form.
- **Technical Risks:** Technical risks concern potential style, implementation, interfacing, testing, and maintenance issues. Technical risks conjointly embody ambiguous specifications, incomplete specifications, dynamic specifications, technical uncertainty, and technical degeneration. Most technical risks occur thanks to the event team's lean information concerning the project.
- **Business Risks:** This type of risk embodies the risks of building a superb product that nobody needs, losing monetary funds or personal commitments, etc.

Benefits of Risk Management

Here are some benefits of risk management:

- Helps protect against potential losses.
- Improves decision-making by considering risks.
- Reduces unexpected expenses.
- Ensures adherence to laws and regulations.

Risk management is important for protecting businesses from potential problems and helping them make better decisions. While it has many advantages, like saving money and keeping things running smoothly, it also has challenges, such as cost and complexity.

Identification

Identifying risk is one of most important or essential and initial steps in risk management process. By chance, if failure occurs in identifying any specific or particular risk, then all other steps that are involved in risk management will not be implemented for that particular risk. For identifying risk, project team should review scope of program, estimate cost, schedule, technical maturity, parameters of key performance, etc. To manage risk, project team or organization are needed to know about what risks it faces, and then to evaluate them.

Methods for Identifying Risks

- Earlier, there were no easy methods available that will surely identify all risks. But nowadays, there are some additional approaches available for identifying risks. Some of approaches for risk identification are given below.

1. **Checklist Analysis:** Checklist Analysis is type of technique generally used to identify or find risks and manage it. The checklist is basically developed by listing items, steps, or even tasks and is then further analysed against criteria to just identify and determine if procedure is completed correctly or not. It is list of risk

that is just found to occur regularly in development of software project. Below is the list of software development risk by Barry Boehm- modified version.

2. **Brainstorming:** This technique provides and gives free and open approach that usually encourages each and everyone on project team to participate. It also results in greater sense of ownership of project risk, and team generally committed to managing risk for given time period of project. It is creative and unique technique to gather risks spontaneously by team members. The team members identify and determine risks in 'no wrong answer' environment.
3. **Casual Mapping:** Causal mapping is method that builds or develops on reflection and review of failure factors in cause and effect of the diagrams. It is very useful for facilitating learning with an organization or system simply as method of project-post evaluation. It is also key tool for risk assessment.
4. **SWOT Analysis:** Strengths-Weaknesses-Opportunities-Threat (SWOT) is very technique and helpful for identifying risks within greater organization context. It is generally used as planning tool for analyzing business, its resources, and also its environment simply by looking at internal strengths and weaknesses and opportunities and threats in external environment.
5. **Flowchart Method:** This method allows for dynamic process to be diagrammatically represented in paper. This method is generally used to represent activities of process graphically and sequentially to simply identify the risk.

5.2 Projection

Projection in software engineering refers to extracting and displaying relevant information from a complex system while hiding unnecessary details. This concept is widely used in database systems, UI/UX design, software architecture, and machine learning to simplify data representation.Projection is essential for optimization, data abstraction, security, and efficient processing in various domains.

Types of Projection

1. Database Projection (SQL Projection)

- In relational databases, projection refers to retrieving specific columns from a table instead of all data.
- It improves query performance and reduces memory usage. Example: SQL query that retrieves only name and email from a User's table:

```
SELECT name, email FROM Users;
```

2. Software Architecture Projection

- In software engineering, projection is used to view different aspects of a system's architecture without modifying it.
- Helps in modular design by focusing on relevant system components.

Example

- Viewing only the security layer of a multi-layered system without exposing business logic.

- Generating UML component diagrams for specific subsystems.

3. UI/UX Projection

- In user interface design, projection refers to displaying only essential UI components based on user roles or preferences.
- Reduces information overload and improves user experience.

Example

- A banking app hides advanced investment options for basic users.
- An admin dashboard shows detailed analytics, while a customer dashboard shows only transactions.

Projection vs. Selection in Databases

Feature	Projection	Selection
Definition	Retrieves specific columns	Retrieves specific rows
SQL Example	SELECT name, age FROM Employees;	SELECT * FROM Employees WHERE age > 30;
Purpose	Reduces data width (fewer fields)	Reduces data length (fewer records)

Conclusion

Projection helps simplify complex systems by focusing on relevant information. 📌 It is widely used in databases, software architecture, UI design, and AI. Improves efficiency, scalability, and user experience in software systems.

5.3 Risk Mitigation, Monitoring, and Management (RMMM) Plan

A risk management technique is usually seen in the software Project plan. This can be divided into Risk Mitigation, Monitoring, and Management Plan (RMMM). In this plan, all works are done as part of risk analysis. As part of the overall project plan project manager generally uses this RMMM plan.

In some software teams, risk is documented with the help of a Risk Information Sheet (RIS). This RIS is controlled by using a database system for easier management of information i.e creation, priority ordering, searching, and other analysis. After documentation of RMMM and start of a project, risk mitigation and monitoring steps will start.

Risk Mitigation

To mitigate this risk, project management must develop a strategy for reducing turnover. The possible steps to be taken are:

- Meet the current staff to determine causes for turnover (e.g., poor working conditions, low pay, competitive job market).
- Mitigate those causes that are under our control before the project starts.
- Once the project commences, assume turnover will occur and develop techniques to ensure continuity when people leave.

- Organize project teams so that information about each development activity is widely dispersed.

Risk Monitoring

As the project proceeds, risk monitoring activities commence. The project manager monitors factors that may provide an indication of whether the risk is becoming more or less likely. In the case of high staff turnover, the following factors can be monitored:

- General attitude of team members based on project pressures.
- Interpersonal relationships among team members.
- Potential problems with compensation and benefits.
- The availability of jobs within the company and outside it.

Risk Management

Risk management and contingency planning assumes that mitigation efforts have failed and that the risk has become a reality. Continuing the example, the project is well underway, and a number of people announce that they will be leaving. If the mitigation strategy has been followed, backup is available, information is documented, and knowledge has been dispersed across the team.

Drawbacks of RMMM

- It incurs additional project costs.
- It takes additional time.
- For larger projects, implementing an RMMM may itself turn out to be another tedious project.
- RMMM does not guarantee a risk-free project, infact, risks may also come up after the project is delivered.

Definitions and terminology

Below are essential terms and definitions related to project management, estimation, and risk management.

Project Management Terminologies

- **Project:** A project is a temporary activity with a beginning and an ending, that establishes objectives. Yet, projects are singular and the form of their impact on the advancement of an establishment's capacities, items, or administrations.
- **Project Management:** Project management is a process whereby skills, knowledge, and tools are used to plan execute, and close project activities by agreed-upon requirements. It requires harmonizing resources, risk management, and the successful implementation of project goals.
- **Project Manager:** The project manager is the person in charge of designing, implementing, and wrapping a project. They manage the project team, so that tasks are completed timely and within budget, intent being to attain success in a particular project.

- **Scope:** The definition of goals and objectives is referred to as scope. It describes the objectives of the project including deliverables and restrictions that lead to goals development for team members throughout their work.
- **Stakeholder:** Stakeholders are those people, who have stakes in an organization and seek to protect them. These include sponsors, team members, and customers. Stakeholder management is key to the project›s success.

Real-World Examples

1. Scope Creep

- **Scenario:** Suppose you are a project manager of software developers. To begin with, the project scope involves building a mobile application that has particular functions. In the course of implementation, stakeholders ask for new features that were not included in the initial deal.
- **Project Management Terminology in Action:** Additional feature requests are a form of scope creep. To deal with this, you should evaluate the effect on schedule and expense, and communicate with stakeholders which can be necessary to change the project plan.

2. Risk Management

- **Scenario:** You manage a construction site for the erection of an office building. So as the project manager, you identify a potential weather delay due to winter.
- **Project Management Terminology in Action:** The risk is the potential for weather-related delays. This danger is controlled by formulating a contingency plan, tracking the weather reports, and liaising with the construction team to prepare for interruptions.

3. Agile Development

- **Scenario:** Your team is completing a software development project using the Agile approach. In a sprint review, the product owner recognizes an alteration in user needs.
- **Project Management Terminology in Action:** In the Agile environment, it is assumed that the user's changing requirements will be accommodated. The team recaptures their situation, makes adjustments to the backlog, and includes any added requirements within another sprint.

Recognizing and utilizing project management language proficiently are essential components of accomplishing projects. These terminologies act as a common language that promotes flexibility in response to change, reduces risks, maximizes resources, and allows for easy interaction.

Quality of Conformance

Quality of Conformance ensures that a product, service, or process strictly follows **design specifications, industry standards, and customer requirements** without deviations. This involves various **processes and activities** aimed at maintaining consistency, reducing defects, and ensuring high-quality output.

Principles of Project Management Process Activities

Project management is the use of methods, tools and processes to effectively plan and execute projects. Successful project management uses teams and resources to complete project tasks within time, cost and scope. The purpose of a project is defined by the client or stakeholders, and the project manager uses project management methods to develop a plan that describes the allocation of resources, tasks, distances and releases required to meet the needs of the participants.

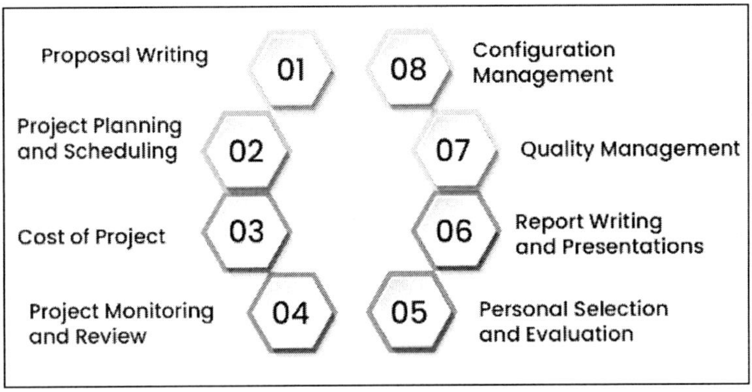

Figure 5.3

1. **Proposal Writing:** Proposal Writing includes
   - A brief analysis of the vital objectives of the project.
   - How the objectives will be achieved and fulfilled.
   - Cost and schedule estimates.
2. **Project Planning and Scheduling:** Project planning includes
   - Identification of activities.
   - Causes (reports, manual) of management.
   - Deliverables for the customer.
3. **Cost of Project** - Project cost represents the sum of all project-related outputs supported by long-term funding. It is important that Project Expenditure is accurately measured as under cost estimates will lead to a lack of funding. Cost of the project includes
   - Estimating the total cost of projects.
4. **Project Monitoring and Review:** Monitoring is an ongoing process and includes
   - Project progress is regularly compared to planned time and cost schedule can be done through informal daily conversations or formal meetings.
     - Reviews include Review of all technological advances in the project is done regularly.
5. **Personal Selection andEvaluation:** Personal selection and evaluation includes
   - Selection of skilled and experienced project staff.
   - Regular monitoring of staff performance.
   - Inexperienced employees can be trained.

6. **Report Writing and Presentations:** The purpose of the presentation is not simply to convey details. After all, the audience at the show can read a written report for themselves. The purpose of the presentation is to 'sell' the ideas contained in this report by urging the audience to act on its recommendations.
    - The project report is written briefly to present before the client & contractor.
7. **Quality Management:** Quality management includes –
    - Quality Assurance
    - Quality Planning
    - Quality Control
8. **Configuration Management:** Configuration is a set of functions designed to control change by identifying work products that can change, establish relationships between them, defined management methods a different kind of these products, controls and set changes auditing and reporting on changes made. It Includes –
    - Identifying work products.
    - Product management and control, testing, change reporting.

Project Management Process Activities Advantages

Whether you run a small business or an established organization, you may not be able to manage all kinds of projects from start to finish. Some projects are very difficult and have strong deadlines or require special skills that your team may not have. A qualified project manager can help you plan and manage the most time-consuming tasks.

Project Management Process Activities Disadvantages

If a project manager does not have the right information or knowledge, there are many problems that can arise. Loss of resources, planning problems, security issues and conflicts between people are major issues in project management.

In conclusion, project management is about finishing up paperwork, learning from mistakes, freeing up resources, checking if the project did what it was supposed to, and having a celebration to mark success.

5.4 Configuration Audit in Project Management

A **Configuration Audit** is a formal evaluation to verify that a project's products, systems, or components conform to their specified requirements, design documentation, and contractual agreements. It is a crucial part of **Configuration Management** and ensures that changes and updates are properly controlled.

1. Types of Configuration Audits

There are two main types of configuration audits:

- Functional Configuration Audit (FCA)
- Physical Configuration Audit (PCA)

Functional Configuration Audit (FCA)

A Functional Configuration Audit (FCA) is a formal review process conducted to verify that a system, product, or component meets all specified functional and performance requirements as outlined in its design documentation. It ensures that the product performs as intended before it is approved for deployment or release.

Purpose

- To confirm that the system functions correctly as per design requirements.
- To verify that all necessary documentation and test results are complete and accurate.
- To ensure that all requirements have been implemented and tested successfully.

Importance of FCA in Project Management

- Ensures Functional Accuracy: Confirms that the product performs as required.
- Reduces Risk: Identifies defects early, preventing costly fixes later.
- Supports Compliance: Meets regulatory and industry standards (ISO, CMMI, etc.).
- Enhances Documentation: Keeps all records updated for future reference.
- Improves Stakeholder Confidence: Provides assurance that the product is ready for use.

Key Takeaway

- A Functional Configuration Audit (FCA) is a critical quality check in project management that verifies whether a system meets all functional requirements before deployment or further testing.

Physical Configuration Audit (PCA)

A Physical Configuration Audit (PCA) is a formal review process that ensures a product's design documentation (e.g., technical drawings, specifications, manuals) matches the actual, physical product. It verifies that the final system has been manufactured, coded, and assembled correctly according to approved design specifications.

Key Aspects of PCA

- **Design vs. Product Validation:** Ensures the physical product matches the approved design.
- **Component & Material Verification:** Checks that the correct parts, materials, and versions are used.
- **Manufacturing & Assembly Review:** Confirms that the product has been built per specifications.
- **Technical Documentation Audit:** Validates blueprints, engineering drawings, bills of materials (BOM), and production records.
- **Configuration Management Compliance:** Ensures that all approved changes are documented and reflected in the final product.

Importance of PCA in Project Management

- Ensures Product Accuracy: Verifies that the final product matches the approved design.
- **Reduces Defects & Rework:** Identifies mismatches early to prevent costly fixes.

- **Enhances Traceability:** Keeps manufacturing and design records up to date.
- **Supports Compliance:** Ensures adherence to industry standards (ISO, CMMI, MIL-STD).
- **Improves Quality Control:** Helps maintain high-quality production standards.
  - **Key Takeaway:** A Physical Configuration Audit (PCA) is essential in project management to verify that the final product conforms to design specifications, preventing defects and ensuring manufacturing consistency.

5.5 Software Quality Assurance

Software Quality Assurance (SQA) is simply a way to assure quality in the software. It is the set of activities that ensure processes, procedures as well as standards are suitable for the project and implemented correctly.Software Quality Assurance is a process that works parallel to Software Development. It focuses on improving the process of development of software so that problems can be prevented before they become major issues. Software Quality Assurance is a kind of Umbrella activity that is applied throughout the software process.

What is Quality?

Quality in a product or service can be defined by several measurable characteristics. Each of these characteristics plays a crucial role in determining the overall quality.

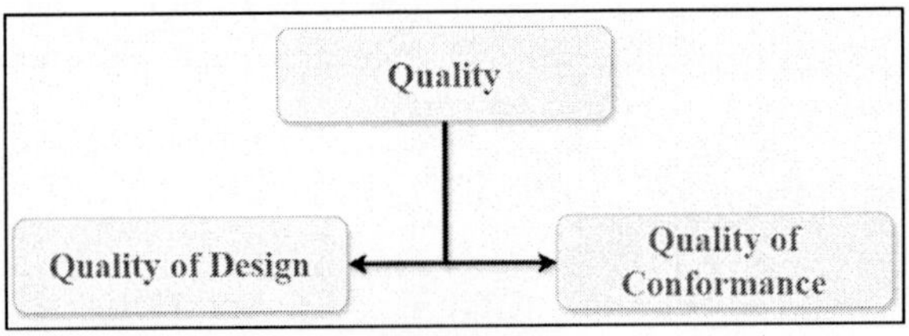

Figure 5.4

5.5.1 Software Quality Assurance (SQA) Encompasses

SQA process Specific quality assurance and quality control tasks (including technical reviews and a multitiered testing strategy) Effective software engineering practice (methods and tools) Control of all software work products and the changes made to them a procedure to ensure compliance with software development standards (when applicable) measurement and reporting mechanisms.

Software Quality Assurance (SQA) Focuses

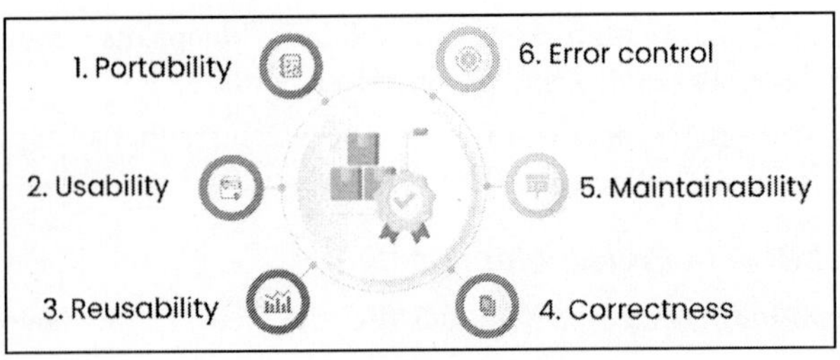

Figure 5.5

- **Software's portability:** Software's **portability** refers to its ability to be easily transferred or adapted to different environments or platforms without needing significant modifications. This ensures that the software can run efficiently across various systems, enhancing its accessibility and flexibility.
- **Software's Usability: Usability** of software refers to how easy and intuitive it is for users to interact with and navigate through the application. A high level of usability ensures that users can effectively accomplish their tasks with minimal confusion or frustration, leading to a positive user experience.
- **Software's Reusability: Reusability** in software development involves designing components or modules that can be reused in multiple parts of the software or in different projects. This promotes efficiency and reduces development time by eliminating the need to reinvent the wheel for similar functionalities, enhancing productivity and maintainability.
- **Software's Correctness: Correctness** of software refers to its ability to produce the desired results under specific conditions or inputs. Correct software behaves as expected without errors or unexpected behaviors, meeting the requirements and specifications defined for its functionality.
- **Software's Maintainability: Maintainability** of software refers to how easily it can be modified, updated, or extended over time. Well-maintained software is structured and documented in a way that allows developers to make changes efficiently without introducing errors or compromising its stability.
- **Software's Error Control: Error control** in software involves implementing mechanisms to detect, handle, and recover from errors or unexpected situations gracefully. Effective error control ensures that the software remains robust and reliable, minimizing disruptions to users and providing a smoother experience overall.

Major Software Quality Assurance (SQA) Activities

- **SQA Management Plan:** Make a plan for how you will carry out the SQA throughout the project. Think about which set of software engineering activities are the best for project. check level of SQA team skills.
- **Set The Check Points:** SQA team should set checkpoints. Evaluate the performance of the project on the basis of collected data on different check points.
- **Measure Change Impact:** The changes for making the correction of an error sometimes re introduces more errors keep the measure of impact of change on project. Reset the new change to check the compatibility of this fix with whole project.
- **Multi testing Strategy:** Do not depend on a single testing approach. When you have a lot of testing approaches available use them.
- **Manage Good Relations:** In the working environment managing good relations with other teams involved in the project development is mandatory. Bad relation of SQA team with programmers team will impact directly and badly on project. Don't play politics.
- **Maintaining records and reports:** Comprehensively document and share all QA records, including test cases, defects, changes, and cycles, for stakeholder awareness and future reference.

- **Reviews software engineering activities:** The SQA group identifies and documents the processes. The group also verifies the correctness of software product.
- **Formalize deviation handling:** Track and document software deviations meticulously. Follow established procedures for handling variances.

Software Quality Assurance (SQA) maintain a most important role in the ensuring the quality, reliability and efficiency of the product. By implementation of these control process which cause the improvement of the software engineering process . SQA gives a higher quality product which help to meet user expectations, its having some drawback also like Cost, time-consuming process, after maintaining the process of the SQA its improved the reliability and maintain the maintenance cost which affect in a future.

Quality Definition

Quality is the degree to which a product, service, or process meets specified requirements and customer expectations. It ensures that the final output is **reliable, efficient, and defect-free** while adhering to industry standards and best practices.Traditionally, a high-quality product is outlined in terms of its fitness of purpose. That is, a high-quality product will specifically be what the users need to try. For code merchandise, the fitness of purpose is typically taken in terms of satisfaction of the wants arranged down within the SRS document.

Though "fitness of purpose" could be a satisfactory definition of quality for some merchandise like an automobile, a table fan, a grinding machine, etc. – for code merchandise, "fitness of purpose" isn't a completely satisfactory definition of quality.

What is Software Quality?

Software Quality shows how good and reliable a product is. To convey an associate degree example, think about functionally correct software. It performs all functions as laid out in the SRS document. But, it has an associate degree virtually unusable program. even though it should be functionally correct, we tend not to think about it to be a high-quality product.

Factors of Software Quality

The modern read of high-quality associates with software many quality factors like the following:

- **Portability:** A software is claimed to be transportable, if it may be simply created to figure in several package environments, in several machines, with alternative code merchandise, etc.
- **Usability:** A software has smart usability if completely different classes of users (i.e. knowledgeable and novice users) will simply invoke the functions of the merchandise.
- **Reusability:** A software has smart reusability if completely different modules of the merchandise will simply be reused to develop new merchandise.
- **Correctness:** Software is correct if completely different needs as laid out in the SRS document are properly enforced.
- **Maintainability:** A software is reparable, if errors may be simply corrected as and once they show up, new functions may be simply added to the merchandise, and therefore the functionalities of the merchandise may be simply changed, etc

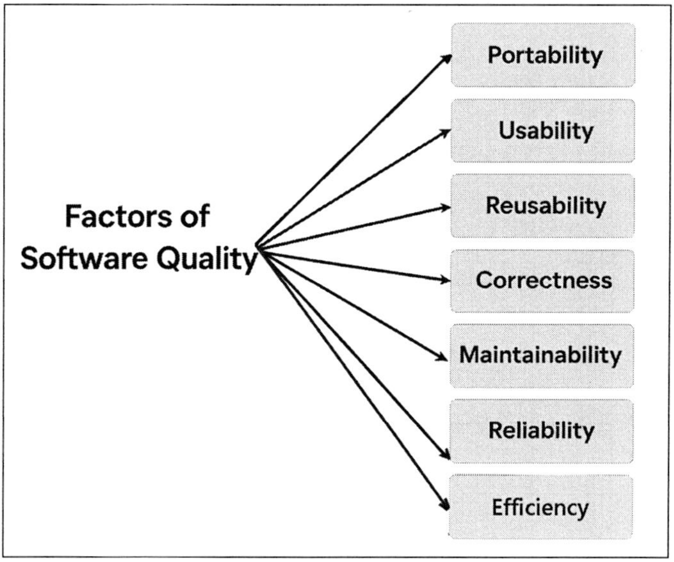

Figure 5.6

- **Reliability:** Software is more reliable if it has fewer failures. Since software engineers do not deliberately plan for their software to fail, reliability depends on the number and type of mistakes they make. Designers can improve reliability by ensuring the software is easy to implement and change, by testing it thoroughly, and also by ensuring that if failures occur, the system can handle them or can recover easily.
- **Efficiency:** The more efficient software is, the less it uses of CPU-time, memory, disk space, network bandwidth, and other resources. This is important to customers in order to reduce their costs of running the software, although with today's powerful computers, CPU time, memory and disk usage are less of a concern than in years gone by.
- Software quality ensures a product is reliable, maintainable, and user-friendly, going beyond just meeting requirements. It involves key factors like portability, usability, correctness, and efficiency. A robust quality management system and continuous improvement processes help achieve these standards. High-quality software is functional, efficient, and adaptable to user needs.

5.6 Quality of Conformance

Quality of Conformance refers to how well a product, service, or system **meets its design specifications** and predefined standards, regardless of whether those specifications are optimal. It is a measure of consistency in **manufacturing, software development, or service delivery** to ensure that defects, deviations, and variations are minimized.

Key Aspects of Quality of Conformance

- **Adherence to Specifications:** Ensuring the product matches design, material, and functional specifications.

- **Manufacturing Consistency:** Reducing variability in production or development processes.
- **Defect Minimization:** Ensuring the product is free from defects or errors through quality control techniques.
- **Process Control & Improvement:** Using tools like **Six Sigma, Statistical Process Control (SPC), and ISO 9001** to maintain conformance.
- **Customer Satisfaction:** A high-quality product that meets specifications ensures fewer failures and enhances customer trust.

Quality of Conformance vs. Quality of Design

Aspect	Quality of Conformance	Quality of Design
Focus	Adherence to design standards	Creating a high-quality product design
Measurement	Consistency in production	Innovation, features, and specifications
Objective	Minimize defects & variations	Maximize functionality & user experiencee
Example	A smartphone's hardware being identical in all units	Designing a smartphone with advanced features

Example

- A luxury car with an advanced design (Quality of Design) may still be considered low-quality if its manufacturing process introduces defects (Quality of Conformance).
- Conversely, an economy car with a basic design can have high Quality of Conformance if it is consistently produced without defects and performs as intended.

Cost and Benefits of Quality

There is cost of activity in every project, it should have business value and software testing is no exception. To optimize its business value, test managers should optimize testing appropriately. There should not be unnecessary testing otherwise it causes unnecessary delays and ends up incurring more costs. Also, there should not be incomplete or too less testing otherwise, there may be a chance of defective products to be handed to the end users. Therefore, software testing should be done appropriately.

- **Cost of Quality:** It is the most established, effective measure of quantifying and calculating the business value of testing. There are four categories to measure cost of quality: Prevention costs, Detection costs, Internal failure costs, and External failure costs.

These are explained as follows below.

- **Prevention costs** include cost of training developers on writing secure and easily maintainable code
- **Detection costs** include the cost of creating test cases, setting up testing environments, revisiting testing requirements.

- **Internal failure costs** include costs incurred in fixing defects just before delivery.
- **External failure costs** include product support costs incurred by delivering poor quality software.

Major parts of total cost are detecting defects and internal failure cost. But, these costs less than external failure costs. That's why testing provides good business value.

Quality Assurance (QA) vs Quality Control (QC)

Quality Assurance (QA) and Quality control (QC) are both important methods in software engineering to get high-quality software. Quality Assurance (QA) prevents software defects or minimizes the number of defects in software before delivery by making sure that proper methods and processes are followed during the software development process. Whereas Quality Control (QC) identifies and fixes the defects or errors that exist after development.

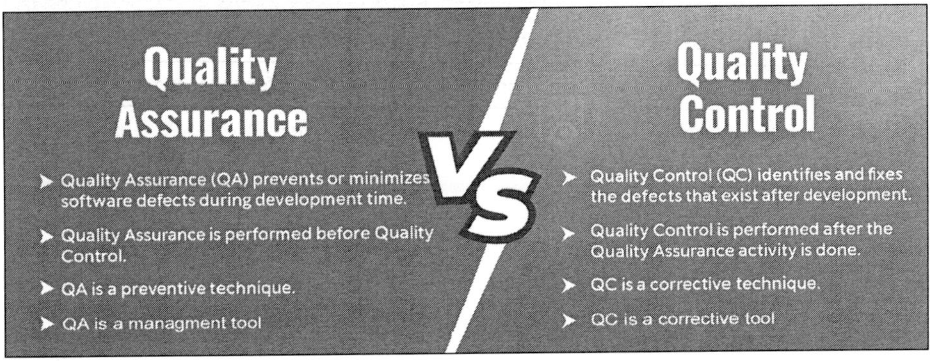

Figure 5.7

What is Quality Assurance (QA)?

Quality assurance is a method of making the software application with fewer defects and mistakes when it is finally released to the end users. Quality Assurance is defined as an activity that ensures the approaches, techniques, methods, and processes designed for the projects are implemented correctly. It recognizes defects in the process. Quality Assurance is completed before Quality Control.

- It focuses on preventing defects.
- It is a proactive process and is preventive in nature.
- It helps to recognize flaws in the process.
- These activities monitor and verify that the processes used to manage and create deliverables have been followed.

Characteristics of Quality Assurance

- **Process-Oriented:** To guarantee constant product quality, it places a strong emphasis on the creation and application of reliable procedures and standards.
- **Proactive Process:** Quality Assurance (QA) tries to prevent errors by enhancing procedures, guaranteeing that quality is integrated into the product from the start.
- **Continuous Improvement**: To improve quality over time, QA includes constant process assessment and improvement.

Examples of QA Activities

- Developing & enforcing quality policies and procedures
- Process audits and compliance checks
- Employee training on best practices
- Supplier quality management

What is Quality Control?

Quality Control is a software engineering process that is used to ensure that the approaches, techniques, methods, and processes designed for the project are followed correctly. Quality control activities operate and verify that the application meet the defined quality standards.

- It focuses on an examination of the quality of the end products and the final outcome rather than focusing on the processes used to create a product.
- It is a reactive process and is detection in nature.
- These activities monitor and verify that the project deliverables meet the defined quality standards.

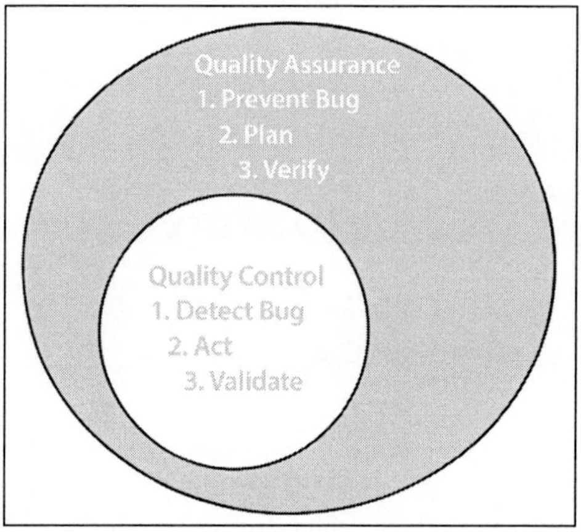

Figure 5.8

Characteristics of Quality Control

- **Reactive Process:** It is the process to find and fix the flaws in the completed product, with focus on finding problems rather than solving them.
- **Defect Identification:** With testing and inspection, the goal is to find the defect as early as possible.
- **Product-oriented:** It entails examining, evaluating, and verifying the product to make sure it satisfies the required standards of quality.

Examples of QC Activities

- **Product testing** (functional, durability, stress testing)
- **Inspection & sampling** in manufacturing
- **Software testing** (unit, integration, system testing)
- **Defect tracking & corrective actions**

Comparison Table: QA vs. QC

Feature	Quality Assurance (QA)	Quality Control (QC)
Purpose	Prevent defects	Detect & fox defects
Approach	Proactive	Reactive
Focus	Process-oriented	Product-oriented
Key Activities	Process audits, training, standardization	Testing, inspection, defect fixing
Methodologies	Six Sigma, ISO 9001, CMMI	SPC, Testing tools, Checklists
Responsibility	QA Team, Process, Owners	QC Team, Testers, Inpectors

Example Scenario

Car Manufacturing

- **QA ensures** that assembly line processes follow strict quality guidelines to minimize defects.
- **QC inspects** finished cars, checking for any defects in paint, engine function, or safety features before shipping.

To follow the high standards in product development, both quality assurance (QA) and quality control (QC) is required. The former prioritizes process improvement as a means of preventing faults, whereas the later concentrates on finding and fixing problems in the finished product. Together, they guarantee that throughout the production cycle, quality is continuously attained and maintained.

Software Cost Estimation

Whenever we develop a software project, main questions that arise in our mind is how much it will cost to develop and how much time it will take for development. These estimates are necessary and needed before initiating development. But main critical problem that arises during software cost estimation is lack of case studies of projects usually created in a well-documented manner.

The software industry has inconsistently defined and explained metrics or atomic units of measure, data from real and actual projects are largely and highly suspect in terms of consistency and comparability. There are many questions as debates among developers and vendors of software cost estimation models and tools.

Nowadays, there are several models available of cost estimation like:

5.7 COCOMO Model

Among all of them, COCOMO model is one of most open and well-documented cost estimation models. At present, most of real-world use of cost models is bottom-up rather than top-down. Below, diagram is given that illustrates and represents predominant practice. The manager of software project defines and describes target cost of software, and after then until target cost can be justified, it manipulates parameters and size.

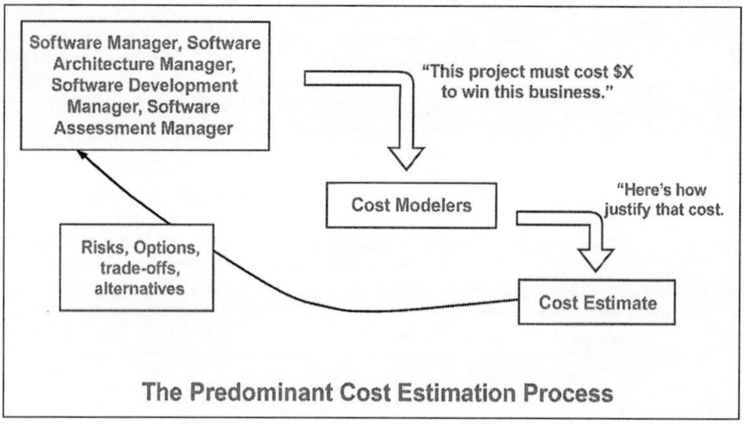

Figure 5.9

The process is described in diagram is very necessary to analyze and predict cost risks and understand sensitivities and trade-offs objectively. It simply forces manager of software project to examine and find out risks associated with achieving target costs and to discuss and explain this gained information with other stakeholders.

Good Software Cost Estimate

Contains

- It is simply conceived i.e. planned and supported by project manager, architecture team, development team, and test team responsible for performing work and task.
- All the stakeholders generally accept it as ambitious but realizable.
- It is based on a well-defined and efficient cost model of software on a credible basis.
- It is also based on a similar project experience database that includes and contains similar processes, relevant technologies, relevant environments, relevant quality requirements, and all similar people.
- It is also defined and explained in much amount of detail so that all of its key risks are simply understood and probability of success is objectively assessed.
- It contains any extra details, supporting documentation or any information that could be relevant to the estimate.
- It stresses how important it is to keep the cost estimates updated and revised on a frequent basis as the project moves forward and new information becomes available.
- Any assumptions that were made throughout the estimation process are documented.

Extrapolating from a good estimate, an ideal estimate would be derived from a mature cost model with an experience base that generally reflects more similar projects that are done by same team with similar mature processes and tools.

Use of Cost Estimation

- One needs to choose and determine how many engineers are required for project to develop and establish a schedule during planning stage.

- While monitoring project's progress, one needs to access whether project is progressing towards achieving goal according to procedure and whether it takes corrective action or not.
- It makes it possible to allocate resources such as labor, tools and supplies in a way that maximizes effectiveness and reduces waste.
- Cost estimates are used as a starting point for talks and agreements between parties when negotiating contracts or project requirements.
- It offers a shared understanding of the financial concerns and facilitates open and honest communication among project stakeholders.
- It affects resource allocation and project duration, that is why the amount of time needed for various project activities is a crucial component in cost assessment.

Example: Using COCOMO for Estimation

COCOMO (Constructive Cost Model) estimates effort and cost based on project size:

Effort (Person-Months) = a × $(KLOC)^b$

Where:

- **KLOC** = Thousands of lines of code
- **a, b** = Constants based on project type (organic, semi-detached, embedded)

For example, if a software project has **50 KLOC** and uses **organic development** (a = 2.4, b – 1.05) the COCOMO formula might give:

Effort = 2.4 × $(50)^{1.05}$ = 153.21 Person-Months

This effort is then converted into **cost** based on salary, overhead, and resources.

COCOMO Model

The Constructive Cost Model (COCOMO) is a software cost estimation model that helps predict the effort, cost, and schedule required for a software development project. Developed by Barry Boehm in 1981, COCOMO uses a mathematical formula based on the size of the software project, typically measured in lines of code (LOC).

What is the COCOMO Model?

The COCOMO Model is a procedural cost estimate model for software projects and is often used as a process of reliably predicting the various parameters associated with making a project such as size, effort, cost, time, and quality.

The key parameters that define the quality of any software product, which are also an outcome of COCOMO, are primarily effort and schedule:

- **Effort:** Amount of labor that will be required to complete a task. It is measured in person-months units.
- **Schedule:** This simply means the amount of time required for the completion of the job, which is, of course, proportional to the effort put in. It is measured in the units of time such as weeks, and months.

Types of Projects in the COCOMO Model

In the COCOMO model, software projects are categorized into three types based on their complexity, size, and the development environment. These types are:

- **Organic:** A software project is said to be an organic type if the team size required is adequately small, the problem is well understood and has been solved in the past and also the team members have a nominal experience regarding the problem.
- **Semi-detached**: A software project is said to be a Semi-detached type if the vital characteristics such as team size, experience, and knowledge of the various programming environments lie in between organic and embedded. The projects classified as Semi-Detached are comparatively less familiar and difficult to develop compared to the organic ones and require more experience better guidance and creativity.
- **Embedded:** A software project requiring the highest level of complexity, creativity, and experience requirement falls under this category. Such software requires a larger team size than the other two models and also the developers need to be sufficiently experienced and creative to develop such complex models.

Detailed Structure of COCOMO Model

Detailed COCOMO incorporates all characteristics of the intermediate version with an assessment of the cost driver's impact on each step of the software engineering process. The detailed model uses different effort multipliers for each cost driver attribute. In detailed COCOMO, the whole software is divided into different modules and then we apply COCOMO in different modules to estimate effort and then sum the effort.

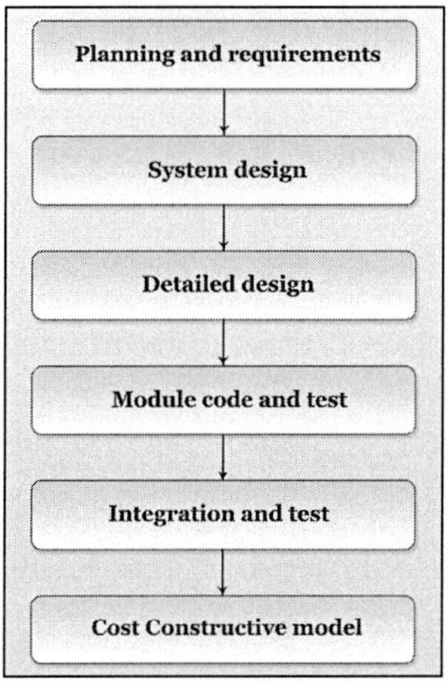

Figure 5.10

- **Planning and requirements:** This initial phase involves defining the scope, objectives, and constraints of the project. It includes developing a project plan that outlines the schedule, resources, and milestones
- **System design:** In this phase, the high-level architecture of the software system is created. This includes defining the system's overall structure, including major components, their interactions, and the data flow between them.
- **Detailed design:** This phase involves creating detailed specifications for each component of the system. It breaks down the system design into detailed descriptions of each module, including data structures, algorithms, and interfaces.

- **Module code and test:** This involves writing the actual source code for each module or component as defined in the detailed design. It includes coding the functionalities, implementing algorithms, and developing interfaces.
- **Integration and test**: This phase involves combining individual modules into a complete system and ensuring that they work together as intended.
- **Cost Constructive model:** The Constructive Cost Model (COCOMO) is a widely used method for estimating the cost and effort required for software development projects.

Different models of **COCOMO** have been proposed to predict the cost estimation at different levels, based on the amount of accuracy and correctness required. All of these models can be applied to a variety of projects, whose characteristics determine the value of the constant to be used in subsequent calculations.

Types of COCOMO Model

There are three types of COCOMO Model:

- Basic COCOMO Model
- Intermediate COCOMO Model
- Detailed COCOMO Model

1. Basic COCOMO Model

The Basic COCOMO model is a straightforward way to estimate the effort needed for a software development project. It uses a simple mathematical formula to predict how many person-months of work are required based on the size of the project, measured in thousands of lines of code (KLOC).

It estimates effort and time required for development using the following expression:

$E = a \times (KLOC)^b$ PM

$T_{dev} = c \times (E)^d$

Person required = Effort/ Time

Where,

E is effort applied in Person-Months

KLOC is the estimated size of the software product indicate in Kilo Lines of Code

T_{dev} is the development time in months

a, b, c are constants determined by the category of software project given in below table.

The above formula is used for the cost estimation of the basic COCOMO model and also is used in the subsequent models.

The constant values a, b, c, and d for the Basic Model for the different categories of the software projects are:

Software Projects	a	b	c	d
Organic	2.4	1.05	2.5	0.38
Semi Detached	3.0	1.12	2.5	0.35
Embedded	3.6	1.20	2.5	0.32

Example of Basic COCOMO Model

Suppose that a Basic project was estimated to be 400 KLOC (kilo lines of code). Calculate effort and time for each of the three modes of development. All the constants value provided in the following table:

Solution

From the above table we take the value of constant a,b,c and d.

- For organic mode,
  - effort = 2.4 × (400)1.05 ≈ 1295 person-month.
  - dev. time = 2.5 × (1295)0.38 ≈ 38 months.
- For semi-detach mode,
  - effort = 3 × (400)1.12 ≈ 2462 person-month.
  - dev. time = 2.5 × (2462)0.35 ≈ 38 months.
- For Embedded mode,

- effort = 3.6 × (400)1.20 ≈ 4772 person-month.
- dev. time = 2.5 × (4772)0.32 ≈ 38 months.

2. Intermediate COCOMO Model

The basic COCOMO model assumes that the effort is only a function of the number of lines of code and some constants evaluated according to the different software systems. However, in reality, no system's effort and schedule can be solely calculated based on Lines of Code. For that, various other factors such as reliability, experience, and Capability. These factors are known as Cost Drivers (multipliers) and the Intermediate Model utilizes 15 such drivers for cost estimation.

Classification of Cost Drivers and their Attributes:

The cost drivers are divided into four categories:

Product Attributes

- Required software reliability extent
- Size of the application database
- The complexity of the product

Hardware Attributes

- Run-time performance constraints
- Memory constraints
- The volatility of the virtual machine environment
- Required turnabout time

The Effort Adjustment Factor (EAF) is employed to enhance the estimates generated by the basic COCOMO model in the following expression:

Intermediate COCOMO Model Equation

$E = a \times (KLOC)^b \times EAF$ PM

$T_{dev} = c \times (E)^d$

Where,

- E is effort applied in Person-Months
- KLOC is the estimated size of the software product indicate in Kilo Lines of Code
- EAF is the Effort Adjustment Factor (EAF) is a multiplier used to refine the effort estimate obtained from the basic COCOMO model.
- T_{dev} is the development time in months
- a, b, c are constants determined by the category of software project given in below table.

The constant values a, b, c, and d for the Basic Model for the different categories of the software projects are:

Software Projects	a	b	c	d
Organic	3.2	1.05	2.5	0.38
Semi Detached	3.0	1.12	2.5	0.35
Embedded	2.8	1.20	2.5	0.32

3. Detailed COCOMO Model

Detailed COCOMO goes beyond Basic and Intermediate COCOMO by diving deeper into project-specific factors. It considers a wider range of parameters, like team experience, development practices, and software complexity. By analyzing these factors in more detail, Detailed COCOMO provides a highly accurate estimation of effort, time, and cost for software projects. It's like zooming in on a project's unique characteristics to get a clearer picture of what it will take to complete it successfully.

Example Use Case:

You are developing a **Semi-Detached** system estimated to have **100 KLOC**.

Using **Basic COCOMO**:

$$\text{Effort} = 3.0 \times (100)^{1.12} = 3.0 \times 126 = 378 \text{ Person-Months}$$

If cost drivers lead to **EAF = 1.2**, then using **Intermediate COCOMO**:

$$\text{Effort} = 3.0 \times (100)^{1.12} \times 1.2 = 453.6 \text{ Person-Months}$$

The COCOMO model provides a structured way to estimate the time, effort, and cost needed for software development based on project size and various influencing factors. It helps project managers and developers plan resources effectively and set realistic timelines and budgets, improving overall project management and success.

Software Maintenance

Software Maintenance refers to the process of modifying and updating a software system after it has been delivered to the customer. This involves fixing bugs, adding new features, and adapting to new hardware or software environments. Effective maintenance is crucial for extending the software's lifespan and aligning it with evolving user needs. It is an essential part of the software development life cycle (SDLC), involving planned and unplanned activities to keep the system reliable and up-to-date. This article focuses on discussing Software Maintenance in detail.

What is Software Maintenance?

Software maintenance is a continuous process that occurs throughout the entire life cycle of the software system.

- The goal of software maintenance is to keep the software system working correctly, efficiently, and securely, and to ensure that it continues to meet the needs of the users.
- This can include fixing bugs, adding new features, improving performance, or updating the software to work with new hardware or software systems.
- It is also important to consider the cost and effort required for software maintenance when planning and developing a software system.
- It is important to have a well-defined maintenance process in place, which includes testing and validation, version control, and communication with stakeholders.

Several Key Aspects of Software Maintenance

- **Bug Fixing:** The process of finding and fixing errors and problems in the software.
- **Enhancements:** The process of adding new features or improving existing features to meet the evolving needs of the users.
- **Performance Optimization:** The process of improving the speed, efficiency, and reliability of the software.
- **Porting and Migration:** The process of adapting the software to run on new hardware or software platforms.
- **Re-Engineering:** The process of improving the design and architecture of the software to make it more maintainable and scalable.
- **Documentation:** The process of creating, updating, and maintaining the documentation for the software, including user manuals, technical specifications, and design documents.
- Several Types of Software Maintenance:
- **Corrective Maintenance:** This involves fixing errors and bugs in the software system.
- **Patching:** It is an emergency fix implemented mainly due to pressure from management. Patching is done for corrective maintenance but it gives rise to unforeseen future errors due to lack of proper impact analysis.
- **Adaptive Maintenance:** This involves modifying the software system to adapt it to changes in the environment, such as changes in hardware or software, government policies, and business rules.
- **Perfective Maintenance**: This involves improving functionality, performance, and reliability, and restructuring the software system to improve changeability.
- **Preventive Maintenance:** This involves taking measures to prevent future problems, such as optimization, updating documentation, reviewing and testing the system, and implementing preventive measures such as backups.

Software maintenance is also an important part of the Software Development Life Cycle (SDLC). To update the software application and do all modifications in software application so as to improve performance is the main focus of software maintenance. Software is a model that runs on the basis of the real world. so, whenever any change requires in the software that means the need for real-world changes wherever possible.

Challenges in Software Maintenance

- **Lack of documentation**: Poorly documented systems can make it difficult to understand how the system works, making it difficult to identify and fix problems.
- **Legacy code:** Maintaining older systems with outdated technologies can be difficult, as it may require specialized knowledge and skills.
- **Complexity:** Large and complex systems can be difficult to understand and modify, making it difficult to identify and fix problems.
- **Changing requirements:** As user requirements change over time, the software system may need to be modified to meet these new requirements, which can be difficult and time-consuming.
- **Interoperability issues:** Systems that need to work with other systems or software can be difficult to maintain, as changes to one system can affect the other systems.
- **Lack of test coverage**: Systems that have not been thoroughly tested can be difficult to maintain as it can be hard to identify and fix problems without knowing how the system behaves in different scenarios.

To overcome these challenges, it is important to have a well-defined maintenance process in place, which includes testing and validation, version control, and communication with stakeholders. It is also important to have a clear and well-defined maintenance plan that includes regular maintenance activities, such as testing, backup, and bug fixing.

System Configuration Management

System Configuration Management (SCM) is an arrangement of exercises that controls change by recognizing the items for change, setting up connections between those things, making/characterizing instruments for overseeing diverse variants, controlling the changes being executed in the current framework, inspecting and revealing/reporting on the changes made.

It is essential to control the changes because if the changes are not checked legitimately then they may wind up undermining a well-run programming. In this way, SCM is a fundamental piece of all project management activities.

- **Processes involved in SCM:** Configuration management provides a disciplined environment for smooth control of work products. It involves the following activities:
- **Identification and Establishment:** Identifying the configuration items from products that compose baselines at given points in time (a baseline is a set of mutually consistent Configuration Items, which has been formally reviewed and agreed upon, and serves as the basis of further development).

  Establishing relationships among items, creating a mechanism to manage multiple levels of control and procedure for the change management system.

- **Version control:** Creating versions/specifications of the existing product to build new products with the help of the SCM system. A description of the version is given below:

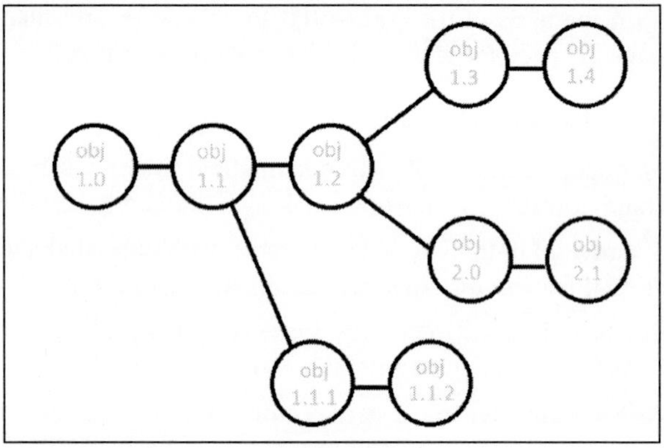

Figure 5.11

Suppose after some changes, the version of the configuration object changes from 1.0 to 1.1. Minor corrections and changes result in versions 1.1.1 and 1.1.2, which is followed by a major update that is object 1.2. The development of object 1.0 continues through 1.3 and 1.4, but finally, a noteworthy change to the object results in a new evolutionary path, version 2.0. Both versions are currently supported.

- **Change control:** Controlling changes to Configuration items (CI). The change control process is explained in Figure below:

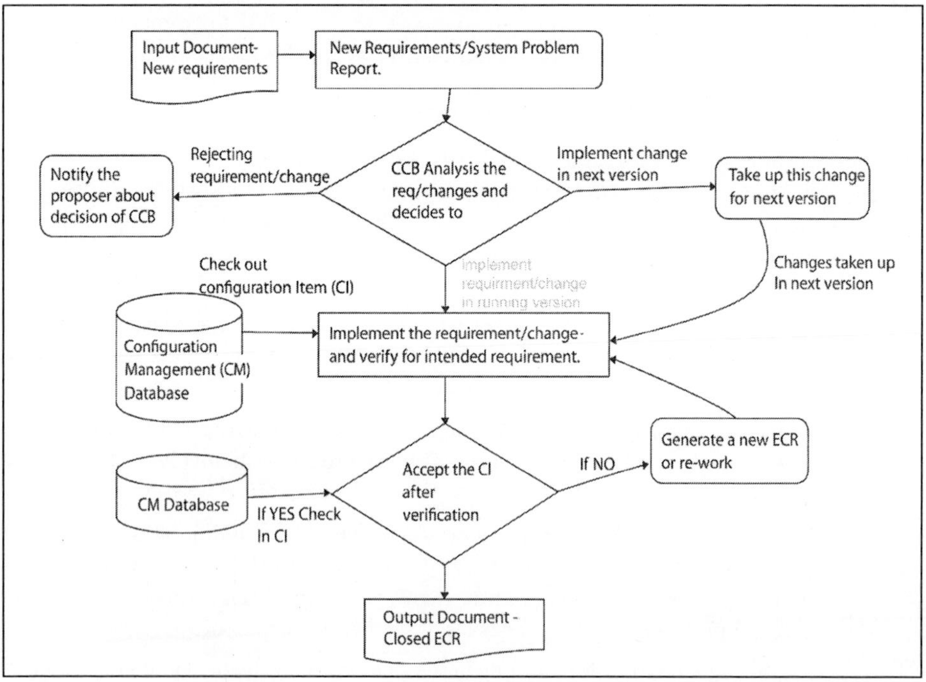

Figure 5.12

A change request (CR) is submitted and evaluated to assess technical merit, potential side effects, the overall impact on other configuration objects and system functions, and the projected cost of the change. The results of the evaluation are presented as a change report, which is used by a change control board (CCB) a person or group who makes a final decision on the status and priority of the change.

An engineering change Request (ECR) is generated for each approved change. Also, CCB notifies the developer in case the change is rejected with proper reason. The ECR describes the change to be made, the constraints that must be respected, and the criteria for review and audit. The object to be changed is "checked out" of the project database, the change is made, and then the object is tested again.

- **Configuration auditing**: A software configuration audit complements the formal technical review of the process and product. It focuses on the technical correctness of the configuration object that has been modified. The audit confirms the completeness, correctness, and consistency of items in the SCM system and tracks action items from the audit to closure.
- **Reporting**: Providing accurate status and current configuration data to developers, testers, end users, customers, and stakeholders through admin guides, user guides, FAQs, Release notes, Memos, Installation Guide, Configuration guides, etc.

System Configuration Management (SCM) is a software engineering practice that focuses on managing the configuration of software systems and ensuring that software components are properly controlled, tracked, and stored.

It is a critical aspect of software development, as it helps to ensure that changes made to a software system are properly coordinated and that the system is always in a known and stable state.

Key Objectives of SCM

- **Control the evolution of software systems:** SCM helps to ensure that changes to a software system are properly planned, tested, and integrated into the final product.
- **Enable collaboration and coordination:** SCM helps teams to collaborate and coordinate their work, ensuring that changes are properly integrated and that everyone is working from the same version of the software system.
- **Provide version control:** SCM provides version control for software systems, enabling teams to manage and track different versions of the system and to revert to earlier versions if necessary.
- **Facilitate replication and distribution:** SCM helps to ensure that software systems can be easily replicated and distributed to other environments, such as test, production, and customer sites.
- SCM is a critical component of software development, and effective SCM practices can help to improve the quality and reliability of software systems, as well as increase efficiency and reduce the risk of errors.

SCM is **essential for modern software development** because it improves collaboration, maintains software integrity, and enhances security. With SCM, teams can **develop, test, and deploy software more efficiently** while minimizing errors.

Version Control Introduction to SCM process Software Reengineering

1. Version Control

What is Version Control?

Version Control is a system that records changes to files over time so developers can track modifications, compare versions, and revert to previous versions if necessary. It is widely used in software development, documentation, and collaborative projects.

Software Configuration Management (SCM) Process

What is SCM?

Software Configuration Management (SCM) is a discipline for systematically managing changes to software to ensure integrity, traceability, and consistency.

5.8 Software Reengineering

What is Software Reengineering?

Software Reengineering is the process of analyzing, modifying, and improving existing software to enhance performance, maintainability, and scalability.

Software Re-engineering is a process of software development that is done to improve the maintainability of a software system. Re-engineering is the examination and alteration of a system to reconstitute it in a new form. This process encompasses a combination of sub-processes like reverse engineering, forward engineering, reconstructing, etc.

What is Re-engineering?

Re-engineering, also known as software re-engineering, is the process of analyzing, designing, and modifying existing software systems to improve their quality, performance, and maintainability.

- This can include updating the software to work with new hardware or software platforms, adding new features, or improving the software's overall design and architecture.
- Software re-engineering, also known as software restructuring or software renovation, refers to the process of improving or upgrading existing software systems to improve their quality, maintainability, or functionality.
- It involves reusing the existing software artifacts, such as code, design, and documentation, and transforming them to meet new or updated requirements.

Objective of Re-engineering

The primary goal of software re-engineering is to improve the quality and maintainability of the software system while minimizing the risks and costs associated with the redevelopment of the system from scratch. Software re-engineering can be initiated for various reasons, such as:

- To describe a cost-effective option for system evolution.
- To describe the activities involved in the software maintenance process.
- To distinguish between software and data re-engineering and to explain the problems of data re-engineering.

Overall, software re-engineering can be a cost-effective way to improve the quality and functionality of existing software systems, while minimizing the risks and costs associated with starting from scratch.

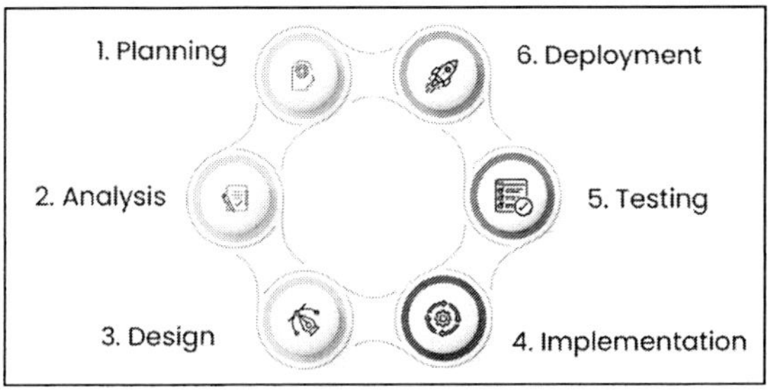

Figure 5.13

- **Planning:** The first step is to plan the re-engineering process, which involves identifying the reasons for re-engineering, defining the scope, and establishing the goals and objectives of the process.
- **Analysis:** The next step is to analyze the existing system, including the code, documentation, and other artifacts. This involves identifying the system's strengths and weaknesses, as well as any issues that need to be addressed.
- **Design:** Based on the analysis, the next step is to design the new or updated software system. This involves identifying the changes that need to be made and developing a plan to implement them.
- **Implementation:** The next step is to implement the changes by modifying the existing code, adding new features, and updating the documentation and other artifacts.
- **Testing:** Once the changes have been implemented, the software system needs to be tested to ensure that it meets the new requirements and specifications.

Software re-engineering is a systematic process aimed at improving existing software systems. It involves analyzing, restructuring, and sometimes rebuilding software to enhance its functionality, adapt it to new requirements, or migrate it to a new platform.

5.9 Reverse Engineering

Software Reverse Engineering is a process of recovering the design, requirement specifications, and functions of a product from an analysis of its code. It builds a program database and generates information from this. This article focuses on discussing reverse engineering in detail.

What is Reverse Engineering?

Reverse engineering can extract design information from source code, but the abstraction level, the completeness of the documentation, the degree to which tools and a human analyst work together, and the directionality of the process are highly variable.

Objective of Reverse Engineering

- **Reducing Costs:** Reverse engineering can help cut costs in product development by finding replacements or cost-effective alternatives for systems or components.
- **Analysis of Security:** Reverse engineering is used in cybersecurity to examine exploits, vulnerabilities, and malware. This helps in understanding of threat mechanisms and the development of practical defenses by security experts.
- **Integration and Customization:** Through the process of reverse engineering, developers can incorporate or modify hardware or software components into pre-existing systems to improve their operation or tailor them to meet particular needs.
- **Recovering Lost Source Code:** Reverse engineering can be used to recover the source code of a software application that has been lost or is inaccessible or at the very least, to produce a higher-level representation of it.
- **Fixing bugs and maintenance**: Reverse engineering can help find and repair flaws or provide updates for systems for which the original source code is either unavailable or inadequately documented.

Reverse Engineering Goals

- **Cope with Complexity:** Reverse engineering is a common tool used to understand and control system complexity. It gives engineers the ability to analyze complex systems and reveal details about their architecture, relationships and design patterns.
- **Recover lost information:** Reverse engineering seeks to retrieve as much information as possible in situations where source code or documentation are lost or unavailable. Rebuilding source code, analyzing data structures and retrieving design details are a few examples of this.
- **Detect side effects:** Understanding a system or component's behavior requires analyzing its side effects. Unintended implications, dependencies, and interactions that might not be obvious from the system's documentation or original source code can be found with the use of reverse engineering.
- **Synthesis higher abstraction**: Abstracting low-level features in order to build higher-level representations is a common practice in reverse engineering. This abstraction makes communication and analysis easier by facilitating a greater understanding of the system's functionality.
- **Facilitate Reuse**: Reverse engineering can be used to find reusable parts or modules in systems that already exist. By understanding the functionality and architecture of a system, developers can extract and repurpose components for use in other projects, improving efficiency and decreasing development time.

Steps of Software Reverse Engineering

- **Collection Information:** This step focuses on collecting all possible information (i.e., source design documents, etc.) about the software.
- **Examining the Information**: The information collected in step-1 is studied so as to get familiar with the system.

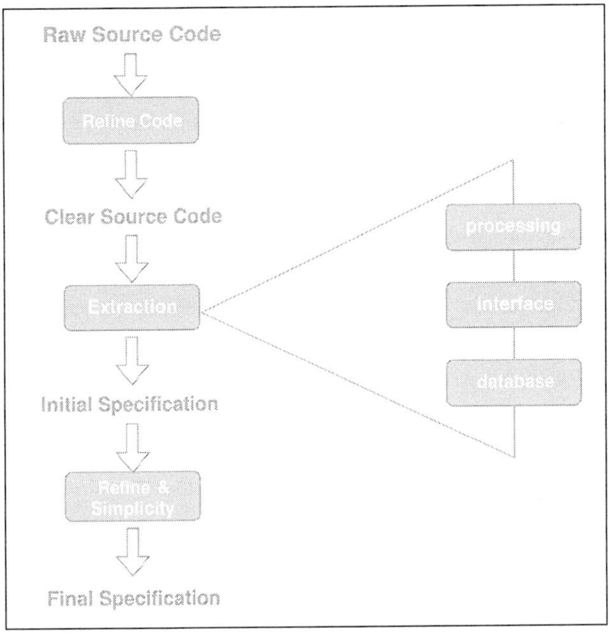

Figure 5.14

- **Extracting the Structure**: This step concerns identifying program structure in the form of a structure chart where each node corresponds to some routine.
- **Recording the Functionality:** During this step processing details of each module of the structure, charts are recorded using structured language like decision table, etc.
- **Recording Data Flow**: From the information extracted in step-3 and step-4, a set of data flow diagrams is derived to show the flow of data among the processes.
- **Recording Control Flow:** The high-level control structure of the software is recorded.
- **Review Extracted Design**: The design document extracted is reviewed several times to ensure consistency and correctness. It also ensures that the design represents the program.
- **Generate Documentation**: Finally, in this step, the complete documentation including SRS, design document, history, overview, etc. is recorded for future use.

Conclusion

- Reverse engineering helps analyze, understand, and improve software systems.
- It is widely used in security, software modernization, and competitive analysis.
- However, it must be conducted ethically and legally to avoid violations.

Restructuring in Software Engineering

Definition: Restructuring in software engineering is the process of improving the internal structure of a software system without changing its external behavior. It is used to enhance readability, maintainability, and performance while preserving functionality.

Why is Restructuring Needed?

- Over time, software systems become complex and difficult to maintain.
- Poorly written code leads to higher maintenance costs.
- Outdated designs and architectures reduce efficiency.
- It helps reduce technical debt and improves scalability.

Types of Restructuring Code Restructuring

Modifying source code to improve readability and efficiency without altering functionality.

- **Techniques:** Removing redundant code Improving variable &function naming Refactoring loops and conditionals Converting monolithic code into modular functions

Benefits of Restructuring

- **Improves Code Maintainability:** Easier for developers to understand and modify.
- **Enhances Performance:** Optimized algorithms and data structures boost efficiency.
- **Reduces Technical Debt:** Minimizes the need for major rewrites later.
- **Extends Software Lifespan:** Makes legacy systems easier to update.
- **Enhances Scalability:** Software can handle growth and increased demand.

Restructuring vs. Refactoring vs. Reengineering

Concept	Definition	Scope	Example
Restructuring	Improves internal structure without changing functionality	Moderate	Splitting large functions into smaller ones
Refactoring	Small, incremental cocde improvements	Small	Renaming variables, optimizing loops
Reengineering	Comprehensive software transformation	Large	Migrating a legacy system to a new framework

Key Takeaway: Restructuring is a **mid-level** improvement approach that **optimizes code, data, and architecture** to keep software **efficient and maintainable** over time.

Forward Engineering

Forward engineering and reverse engineering are two approaches to software development, with different goals and processes. Forward engineering involves creating new software systems from scratch using given requirements and design specifications. It focuses on building new applications through a structured process of analysis, design, implementation, and testing. Reverse engineering, on the other hand, involves analyzing and understanding existing software to extract its design, structure, and functionality.

What is Forward Engineering?

Forward Engineering is a method of creating or making an application with the help of the given requirements. Forward engineering is also known as Renovation and Reclamation.

Forward engineering requires high proficiency skills. It takes more time to construct or develop an application. Forward engineering is a technique of creating high-level models or designs to make complexities and low-level information. Therefore, this kind of engineering has completely different principles in numerous packages and information processes.

Characteristics of Forward Engineering

- Forward engineering is a variety of engineering that has different principles in numerous package and information processes.
- Forward engineering is vital in IT as a result of it represents the 'normal' development process.
- Forward engineering deals with the conversion of business processes, services, and functions into applications.
- In this method, the business model is developed first. Then, a top-down approach is followed to urge the package from the model developed.
- Forward engineering tools are accustomed to moving from implementation styles and logic to the event of supply code.
- It essentially permits the user to develop a business model which may then be translated into data system components.

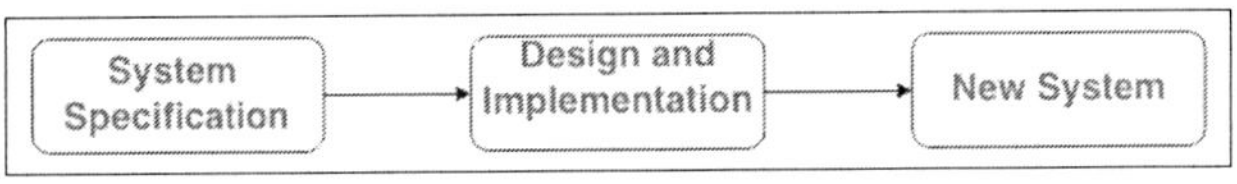

Figure 5.15

Why is Forward Engineering Important?

- Ensures structured and organized software development
- Reduces errors by following predefined specifications
- Improves maintainability and scalability
- Supports modern technology integration

Forward Engineering vs. Reverse Engineering vs. Reengineering

Concept	Definition	Direction	Example
Forward Engineering	Developing software from design to implementation	Design → Code	Writing a new application based on UML diagrams
Reverse Enginreering	Extracting design and specifications from existing code	Code → Design	Analyzing leagacy code to understand its structure
Reengineering	Modifying and improving an existing system	Code → Improved Code	Migrating an old software system to a new platform

Key Takeaway: Forward Engineering **ensures structured software development** by following a step-by-step approach from **design to deployment**.

◆◆◆

This page is intentionally left blank!